IN GOD WE TRUST

PRESIDENTS

Smithsonian | Collins
An Imprint of HarperCollinsPublishers

FOR YOUR INFORMATION

President John F. Kennedy gave the State of the Union address before Congress in January 1963. Ten months later, Vice President Lyndon Johnson, top left, took office when Kennedy was assassinated.

Special thanks to James G. Barber, Historian, National Portrait Gallery, Smithsonian Institution, for his invaluable contribution to this book.

This book was created by **jacob packaged goods LLC** (www.jpgglobal.com):
Written by: Gary Drevitch
Creative: Ellen Jacob, Dawn Camner, Sarah L. Thomson, Andrea Curley, Louise Jacob, Brad McMahon

Photo credits: **pages 2–3, 8** (presidential seal), **18 top and bottom, 19 middle, 23 bottom, 26 bottom, 27 bottom, 28 bottom, 32 bottom, 44 bottom, 45 middle and bottom, 49 bottom, 50 top, 53 middle, 54–55, 55 inset, 56 top, 58 top, 59 middle, 60 top, 63 inset:** The Granger Collection; **page 1:** John F. Kennedy Presidential Library; **pages 6–7:** APImages, **pages 8–9:** George Bush Presidential Library; **pages 10–11:** APImages; **page 12 inset:** White House Historical Association (White House Collection); **pages 12–13:** Eric Long © Smithsonian Institution; **page 14:** APImages; **page 15:** APImages; **page 16:** NPG.80.115, National Portrait Gallery, Smithsonian Institution; **pages 16–17:** Harry T. Peters "America on Stone" Collection, National Museum of American History, Behring Center, Smithsonian Institution; **page 19 top:** NPG.75.52, National Portrait Gallery, Smithsonian Institution; **page 19 bottom:** White House Historical Association (White House Collection); **page 20 top:** NPG.82.97, National Portrait Gallery, Smithsonian Institution, and Monticello, Thomas Jefferson Foundation; **page 21:** Monticello/Thomas Jefferson Foundation, Inc.; **page 22 top:** NPG.68.50, National Portrait Gallery, Smithsonian Institution; **page 23 top:** NPG.70.59, National Portrait Gallery, Smithsonian Institution; **page 24 top:** NPG.69.20, National Portrait Gallery, Smithsonian Institution; **page 25 top:** NPG.65.78, National Portrait Gallery, Smithsonian Institution; **page 26 top:** NPG.76.104, National Portrait Gallery, Smithsonian Institution; **page 27 top:** NPG.67.5, National Portrait Gallery, Smithsonian Institution; **page 28 top:** NPG.70.23, National Portrait Gallery, Smithsonian Institution; **page 30 top:** NPG.76.7, National Portrait Gallery, Smithsonian Institution; **page 30 middle:** NPG.71.47, National Portrait Gallery, Smithsonian Institution; **page 30 bottom:** © E. R. Degginger/Dembinsky Associates; **page 31 top:** NPG.77.55, National Portrait Gallery, Smithsonian Institution; **page 32 top:** NPG.65.49, National Portrait Gallery, Smithsonian Institution; **page 33 top:** NPG.65.48, National Portrait Gallery, Smithsonian Institution; **page 34 top:** NPG.65.50, National Portrait Gallery, Smithsonian Institution; **page 37 top:** NPG.86.213, National Portrait Gallery, Smithsonian Institution; **page 37 middle:** National Museum of American History, Behring Center, Smithsonian Institution; **page 38 top:** NPG.70.16, National Portrait Gallery, Smithsonian Institution; **page 40 top:** NPG.65.25, National Portrait Gallery, Smithsonian Institution; **page 41 top:** NPG.67.62, National Portrait Gallery, Smithsonian Institution; **page 42 top:** NPG.77.229, National Portrait Gallery, Smithsonian Institution; **page 44 top:** NPG.77.229, National Portrait Gallery, Smithsonian Institution; **pages 45 top:** NPG.69.34, National Portrait Gallery, Smithsonian Institution; **page 46 top:** NPG.68.28, National Portrait Gallery, Smithsonian Institution; **page 48 top:** NPG.72.25, National Portrait Gallery, Smithsonian Institution; **page 49 top:** NPG.65.42, National Portrait Gallery, Smithsonian Institution; **page 51 top:** NPG.66.21, National Portrait Gallery, Smithsonian Institution; **page 52 top:** NPG.65.13, National Portrait Gallery, Smithsonian Institution; **page 53 top:** NPG.68.24, National Portrait Gallery, Smithsonian Institution; **page 54:** NPG.68.49, National Portrait Gallery, Smithsonian Institution; **page 57 top:** NPG.70.11, National Portrait Gallery, Smithsonian Institution; **page 59 top:** NPG.65.63, National Portrait Gallery, Smithsonian Institution; **page 61 top:** NPG.68.14, National Portrait Gallery, Smithsonian Institution; **page 62 top:** NPG.72.2, National Portrait Gallery, Smithsonian Institution; **page 63:** APImages; **page 64 top:** NPG.87.245, National Portrait Gallery, Smithsonian Institution; **page 64 middle and bottom:** Gerald R. Ford Presidential Library; **page 65 top:** © Estate of Robert Templeton, NPG.84.154, National Portrait Gallery, Smithsonian Institution; **page 65 middle right:** APImages; **page 65 middle left:** Jimmy Carter Library; **page 66 top:** © Henry C. Casselli, Jr., NPG.90.79, National Portrait Gallery, Smithsonian Institution; **page 66 bottom:** Ronald Reagan Library; **page 67:** Ronald Reagan Library; **page 68 top:** NPG.95.120, National Portrait Gallery, Smithsonian Institution; **page 68 middle:** George Bush Presidential Library Foundation, Chandler Arden, photographer; **page 68 bottom:** George Bush Presidential Library; **page 69 top:** NPG.95.107, National Portrait Gallery, Smithsonian Institution; **page 69 middle:** William J. Clinton Presidential Library; **page 69 bottom:** APImages; **page 70 all:** William J. Clinton Presidential Library; **page 71 top:** White House Historical Association; **page 71 middle and bottom:** APImages; **page 73 bottom:** White House Historical Association (White House Collection); **page 74:** Dayton Barber; all others: Library of Congress

The name of the Smithsonian, Smithsonian Institution and the sunburst logo are trademarks of the Smithsonian Institution. Collins is an imprint of HarperCollins Publishers.

Library of Congress Cataloging-in-Publication Data
Presidents FYI. — 1st ed.
    p.   cm.
  "Smithsonian."
  Includes bibliographical references and index.
  ISBN 978-0-06-089992-9 (trade bdg.) — ISBN 978-0-06-089991-2 (pbk.)
  1. Presidents—United States—Biography—Juvenile literature. 2. Presidents—United States—Juvenile literature. I. Smithsonian Institution.
E176.1.P84 2008   2007032451   973.09'9—dc22   CIP   AC

1 2 3 4 5 6 7 8 9 10
❖
First Edition

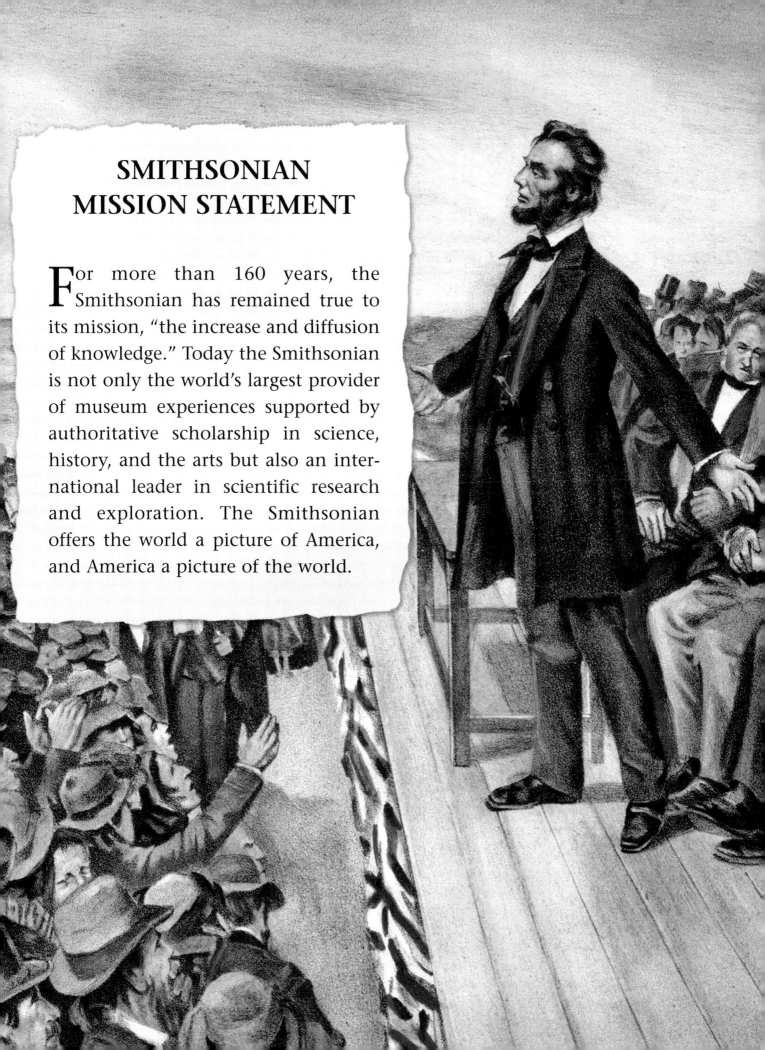

SMITHSONIAN
MISSION STATEMENT

For more than 160 years, the Smithsonian has remained true to its mission, "the increase and diffusion of knowledge." Today the Smithsonian is not only the world's largest provider of museum experiences supported by authoritative scholarship in science, history, and the arts but also an international leader in scientific research and exploration. The Smithsonian offers the world a picture of America, and America a picture of the world.

Contents

What Does the President Do?

Each new president must recite the oath of office, which states:

*I do solemnly swear that I will faithfully execute the office of President of the United States, and will to the best of my ability, preserve, protect and defend the **Constitution** of the United States.*

So how exactly does a president do that?

Commander in Chief

The president defends the United States in his or her role as commander in chief of the army, navy, air force, and marines. The president can also order National Guard troops to active duty to help states facing disasters, or to defend the country in war. The president chooses the secretary of defense and top leaders for each branch of the military. During wars, the president helps make military plans; but no president can declare war on another country. Only **Congress** can do that.

World Leader

The president represents the United States to other countries around the world. The president can meet with other world leaders and make **treaties** and trade deals, but Congress must approve those agreements.

Checks and Balances

The president cannot run the country alone. There is a system of **checks and balances** written into the U.S. Constitution to make sure that no one branch of government—not Congress, not the Supreme Court, and not the president—gets too powerful.

Only Congress can make laws, but the president can **veto**, or reject, new laws. However, Congress can overturn a presidential veto if two-thirds of its members vote to do so. The president also suggests new laws to Congress and can set several kinds of rules and regulations—such as rules for making school lunches healthier or limiting what people can do inside national parks. But those rules and regulations can be rejected by the judges of the Supreme Court. Choosing new Supreme Court justices is another presidential power, although the **Senate** must also approve those judges.

Presidential Power

Despite these limits, the president is still the most important person in the U.S. government. Presidents can set new directions for the country, inspire citizens to change the way they live, and lead the nation through wars that can cost thousands of lives. Decisions made by the president affect millions of people every day. No job in the world has more responsibility—or pressure.

Bill Clinton, the forty-second president, took the oath of office before making his inaugural address to the nation on January 20, 1993.

Cabinet Builder

The president is the head of the government's **executive branch**, and he or she runs it with the help of a team of advisers known as the **cabinet**. Cabinet members, also known as secretaries, are appointed by the president and help run important parts of the government. Cabinet positions include, among others, the secretary of education, who helps set standards for the country's schools; the secretary of defense, who helps run the military; the secretary of the interior, who helps manage the government's land and parks; and the secretary of state, who is in charge of relationships with foreign countries. The cabinet holds regular meetings at which the secretaries give advice to the president.

George H. W. Bush was a navy pilot, a businessman, a member of Congress, the U.S. ambassador to the United Nations, a professor, and the vice president before he was elected president.

The official seal, or symbol, of the president of the United States features an eagle surrounded by fifty stars, which stand for each of the fifty states. The eagle holds an olive branch, showing the country's hopes for peace—and arrows, showing its readiness for war.

As soon as you turn thirty-five years old, you will be old enough to be president, as long as you were born in the United States and have lived here for at least fourteen years. Before they became presidents, George Washington and James Madison helped make these rules part of the U.S. Constitution.

Only a few Americans are forbidden by law from becoming president. Among them are presidents who have already been elected twice. This has been the law since 1951. Just one president in history served more than two terms: Franklin Roosevelt was elected four times in a row, beginning in 1932; but he died early in his fourth term, in 1945.

You don't have to be a member of a **political party** to become president, but it's been more than 150 years since someone who wasn't a member of the Democratic or Republican Party has been elected. It helps to have some experience in government, too. Out of our forty-three presidents, nineteen were state governors, and fourteen were vice presidents. Beginning with Washington, twenty-one served in the U.S. military.

Politics and the military aren't the only careers presidents have pursued. Several were farmers, and two-thirds have been lawyers. At least twelve worked as teachers sometime before they were elected.

No matter what careers presidents held before they ran for the office, when they became candidates, they all had one task in common: working hard to earn people's votes.

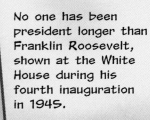

No one has been president longer than Franklin Roosevelt, shown at the White House during his fourth inauguration in 1945.

How Does a President Get Elected?

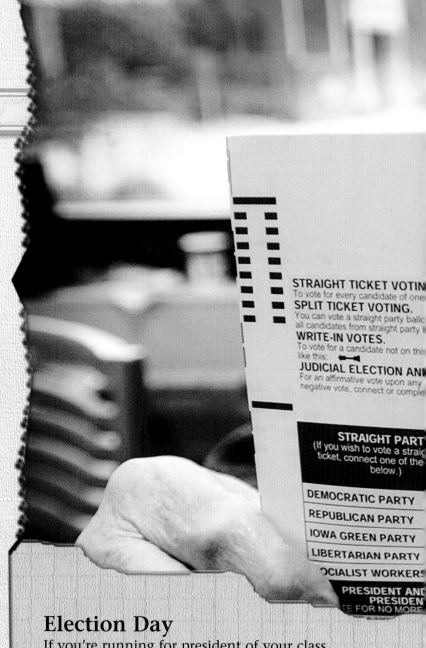

Primary Season

The first step in being elected president is becoming your party's chosen candidate, or **nominee**. As early as two years before a national election, some members of each party begin to campaign, trying to convince people to vote for them. Later, states hold **primary elections**, in which Democrats and Republicans vote for candidates. Then, a few months before the election, each party holds a national meeting, or **convention**, where their members officially select nominees for president and vice president. The presidential nominee is almost always the candidate who wins the most primary elections.

Third Parties

No one but a Democrat or a Republican has won a presidential election since 1848. But candidates from other parties, or **third-party candidates**, have received millions of votes in some elections. Still, no third-party candidate has won an electoral vote since 1968. If any candidate were to receive enough electoral votes to keep any other candidate from winning 270, the election would have to be decided in the **House of Representatives**.

Election Day

If you're running for president of your class, everyone votes, and whoever gets the most votes is the winner. Presidential elections don't work that way. If 100 million people vote and you get 52 million votes, you may not win. In fact, you could lose by a landslide.

When American leaders met in Philadelphia in 1787 to write the new country's constitution, they considered allowing the members of Congress to elect the president. But they decided that under that system, presidents would follow Congress's ideas instead of their own. Still, the writers of the Constitution did not want to let the people elect presidents directly, either. They feared that voters might not make smart choices.

Instead, they decided that presidents would be elected by a special group of people called electors.

10

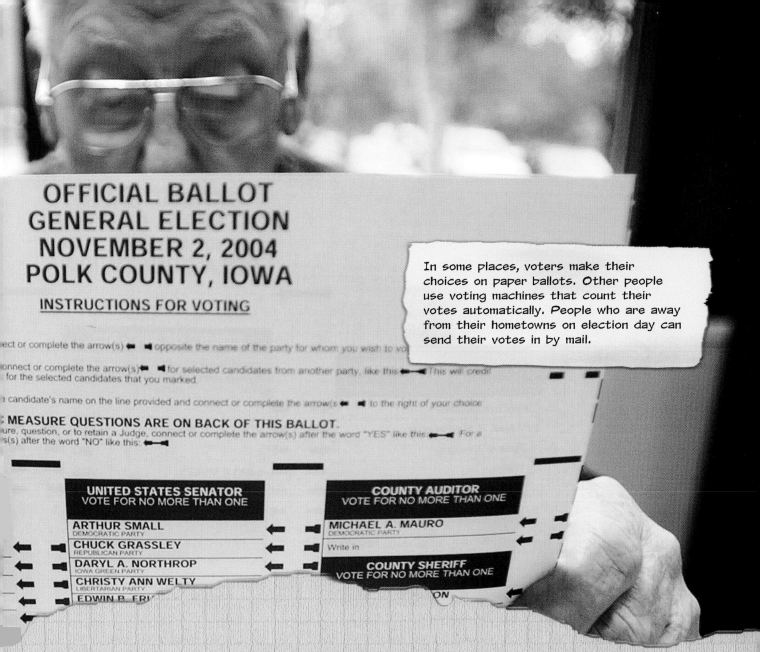

OFFICIAL BALLOT
GENERAL ELECTION
NOVEMBER 2, 2004
POLK COUNTY, IOWA

INSTRUCTIONS FOR VOTING

In some places, voters make their choices on paper ballots. Other people use voting machines that count their votes automatically. People who are away from their hometowns on election day can send their votes in by mail.

These electors made up the **Electoral College**. At first, electors were chosen by individual state's legislatures, but soon every state began allowing people to choose electors directly. Each state has a number of electors equal to its number of U.S. senators plus its number of U.S. representatives. Since the states with the most people have the most representatives, they also get the most electoral votes. California has 55 votes, while Vermont has only 3. The District of Columbia also has 3 electoral votes. The total number of electors is 538, which means that a candidate must collect 270 electoral votes to win the election.

Every four years, the Tuesday following the first Monday in November is election day. On that day most people think they're choosing a president, but they're actually choosing electors who have promised to vote for a candidate. In most states, electors are required by law to support the candidate who won the popular vote in that state, and it is extremely rare for an elector from any state to vote for anyone else. A candidate could win the popular vote in California by just 100 people, but still get all of its 55 electoral votes.

Several candidates have lost presidential elections even though they received more votes than their opponents. Al Gore received about 500,000 more votes than George W. Bush in 2000 but lost the Electoral College vote, 271–266. Some Americans would like to change the system so that the winner of the national popular vote would always become president.

The White House and its gardens, trees, and lawns cover eighteen acres, which are cared for by the thirteen members of the White House grounds crew.

Burning of the White House

In 1814, during the War of 1812 with Great Britain, enemy soldiers attacked Washington, D.C. When the British reached the mansion, they set it on fire, leaving only the stone walls standing. Madison ordered that the house be rebuilt exactly as it had been.

As President Calvin Coolidge walked by the White House one night with a U.S. senator, the senator joked, "I wonder who lives there!" The president answered, "Nobody. They just come and go."

A New Home

The first president, George Washington, ran the nation from New York City, until the government decided to move the capital closer to the center of the country. (At the time, the United States was made up only of states along the East Coast.) The government moved to Philadelphia and remained based there while a new capital was built in the District of Columbia, a large area of empty land on the border between Virginia and Maryland. Washington never got to live in the White House. In 1800, John Adams became the first president to move in, even though the mansion wasn't completely finished. President Thomas Jefferson ordered the tan building to be painted white, but the president's home wasn't officially called the White House until 1901.

A New House

Over the years, presidents added improvements to the White House, such as indoor plumbing, telephone lines, and electricity. The Oval Office, which really is shaped like an oval, was part of an addition built while William Taft was in office. It is still where presidents work today. A famous rose garden was planted in 1913, while Woodrow

Wilson was president. In 1933, an indoor swimming pool was built for Franklin Roosevelt to exercise his paralyzed legs.

By 1948, however, the building was falling apart. The walls were cracked and the wooden beams were weak. A piano leg even crashed through one of the floors! Harry Truman convinced Congress to completely rebuild the house, and volunteered to move out while the work was done. The original stone walls were untouched; but the inside of the house was completely rebuilt. The White House we know today was really built between 1949 and 1952, even though it looks almost the same as it did before.

Inside the White House

Today's White House has six levels, with 132 rooms, 35 bathrooms, and 412 doors. The president's family may use the house's pool, movie theater, and bowling alley. The massive State Dining Room has space for 140 guests, but the biggest room in the house is the East Room, where the president welcomes large groups of visitors and where concerts take place. The president works in the Oval Office in the building's West Wing. An American flag and the presidential flag stand behind his desk. Special guests of the president sometimes stay in the famous Lincoln Bedroom on the second floor, but Abraham Lincoln never slept there. It was his office.

Living Like a President

The daily life of a U.S. president isn't much like yours. For one thing, the president lives—and works—in one of the country's biggest houses, sharing space with a staff of cooks, assistants, and tour guides.

The president never appears in public without Secret Service agents close by.

The Secret Service

Harry Truman called the White House "a glamorous prison." Even when the president is alone in a White House office or bedroom, armed Secret Service guards are always close by. The Secret Service, whose agents are part of the Treasury Department, has protected presidents full-time since 1902. Congress requested the protection after William McKinley was shot and killed in 1901.

Air Force One

Presidents also travel differently from most people. They hardly ever drive their own cars. Instead, Secret Service agents drive presidents and their families in specially protected armored cars. The president usually travels in a motorcade, with Secret Service agents riding in vehicles in front of and behind his car. When the president leaves Washington, he flies in *Air Force One*, a special Boeing 747 jet with large offices for the president and his or her staff, and seats for some TV and newspaper reporters. The plane has a shower and dressing room, along with two kitchens and a medical office. For trips near Washington, the president often flies in a special helicopter named *Marine One*.

Presidential Pay

The president earns $400,000 per year. Since presidents don't pay rent to live in the White House and don't have to buy furniture, groceries, or gas for their cars, they don't usually spend their own money for household items. Presidents do pay for some things, such as snacks and dry cleaning, but some of that money comes out of a $50,000-per-year expense account, which each president receives along with his or her salary.

Growing Up in the White House

Several presidents have shared the White House with their children and tried to make the kids' days in the country's most famous home as normal and fun as possible. The family's upstairs rooms are off-limits to White House visitors so the parents and children can have some privacy. Few White House children had as much fun as Abraham Lincoln's son Thomas, known as Tad, who once shot his toy cannon at the closed door of the room in which a cabinet meeting was being held. Theodore Roosevelt's young sons and their friends called themselves "the White House gang." Among their many pranks, they once reportedly attacked a portrait of Andrew Jackson with spitballs. People who visited John F. Kennedy in the Oval Office often found his son, John Jr., playing under the president's desk. And Jimmy Carter built a tree house for his young daughter, Amy, on the South Lawn of the White House. When she had friends over for slumber parties, Secret Service agents stood guard under the tree.

John F. Kennedy Jr. played under his father's desk in 1963. His sister, Caroline, had a pony named Macaroni that enjoyed walking through the White House gardens.

George Washington
1ST PRESIDENT
1789–1797

BORN IN VIRGINIA IN 1732; DIED IN 1799

As the general in charge of all American troops in the Revolutionary War, George Washington did not win all of his battles. But he made bold decisions that helped win the war. His boldest move may have come on Christmas Day 1775. After a series of losses for the patriots, it seemed as if Great Britain was close to victory. Then, in the middle of the night, Washington led 2,400 troops across the icy Delaware River to Trenton, New Jersey. They surprised the enemy there and won an important victory that kept the war going.

His Country Called

Washington never wanted to be president. But when the Electoral College voted for the first time, in 1789, he was its unanimous choice. Although he had his doubts, he accepted. In 1792, Washington was the unanimous choice once more. Still popular, he could have been elected again in 1796. But he believed presidents should only be allowed to serve two terms, so he retired from the job. It would be almost 150 years before any president would serve more than two terms.

King George?

Although America had just fought a war so it could be free from royal rule, some people thought Washington should have become king instead of president. Fortunately, he disagreed. He and his wife, Martha Washington, tried hard to make sure that people knew that the president and First Lady were not above any other Americans. Still, visitors often called Martha "Lady Washington."

Staying Out of It

In 1793, Great Britain and France went to war. Some Americans felt the United States should take France's side since the French had helped them win the Revolutionary War. Others favored the British. Washington, the former general, knew that the young country wasn't strong enough to fight against either country. He declared that the United States would stay out of the war altogether.

This renowned painting of Washington crossing the Delaware has a famous mistake: in 1775, the first American flag hadn't been made yet!

Not What You Think

Many stories about George Washington were created over the years. A lot of them aren't true. For example, there's a famous story about Washington's honesty, which begins with his chopping down his father's cherry tree. When his father asked him who had chopped down his favorite tree, young George confessed, "I cannot tell a lie." The events in the story never happened. It was one of several myths written by Mason Weems in his popular 1800 book about Washington's life.

17

George Washington

The first cabinet included Thomas Jefferson, second from left, who handled foreign affairs for Washington, right.

The First Cabinet

The U.S. government was a lot smaller in 1789 than it is today. Washington's cabinet had only four secretaries: foreign affairs (now called state), war (now called defense), the treasury, and justice. The secretary of foreign affairs, Thomas Jefferson, and the secretary of the treasury, Alexander Hamilton, often disagreed about the powers of the president. Hamilton believed that the president had "implied" powers, meaning that unless the Constitution said a president couldn't do something, he could do it. Jefferson disagreed. He worried about the country's central government getting too strong. But Washington usually sided with Hamilton, and the office of the president became stronger.

A Capital Deal

Jefferson also disagreed with Hamilton about whether the government should have a central bank for producing paper money. To win his support, a deal was made: Jefferson would support the bank if the nation's capital was moved from New York City to a new site on the border between Maryland and Virginia,

Jefferson's home state. President Washington and his government moved from New York to Philadelphia where they remained while the new capital city, Washington, was being built.

Home at Last

After two terms as president, Washington wanted nothing more than to return home to Mount Vernon, his 8,000-acre farm in Virginia. But he didn't find peace and quiet there. Hundreds of visitors came to Mount Vernon each year to meet America's most famous man.

A Brave First Lady

The lives of Washington and his family did not need to be exaggerated. Martha Washington, for example, took long and dangerous trips across the country during the Revolutionary War, following her husband and his troops from camp to camp. She helped to care for injured troops, as did many other soldiers' wives at the time.

Washington died in his mansion, Mount Vernon, in 1799.

***BORN IN MASSACHUSETTS IN 1735;
DIED IN 1826***

John Adams was the first president to live in the White House. On his second night in the mansion, Adams wrote, "May none but honest and wise Men ever rule under this roof." The roof was finished, but much of the rest of the building wasn't. First Lady Abigail Adams hung the family's laundry in the unfinished space that is today the elegant East Room.

"Remember the Ladies"

Adams was often away from home on government business, so his wife, Abigail, ran the family farm and raised their four children, including their son John Quincy, who would later become president. She also wrote as many as three letters a day to her husband, her "dearest friend." In one letter she urged John, as the president, to support rights for women. "Remember the ladies," she told him. Years later, leaders of the movement for women's rights would remember Mrs. Adams's words.

Building the Navy

While Adams was president, Great Britain and France were at war. The French often attacked American ships on the Atlantic Ocean to keep them from trading with the British. Many Americans wanted Adams to declare war, but he knew the United States did not have enough ships to defeat France in sea battles. In 1800, he agreed to a peace **treaty** with France instead. But he also ordered our country to build more warships so the United States would be prepared for war in the future.

The USS Constitution began sailing for President Adams in 1797.

Today, the East Room of the White House is an elegant party space. During its construction, the Adamses hung their laundry there.

Thomas Jefferson
3RD PRESIDENT
1801–1809

BORN IN VIRGINIA IN 1743; DIED IN 1826

Thomas Jefferson was trained as a lawyer, spoke six languages, played the violin, and was an inventor and an architect. He designed his own Virginia home, Monticello, and in its day, his library of 6,500 books was one of America's largest. How did he find time to do it all? As he once said, "It is wonderful how much may be done if we are always doing."

"Life, Liberty and the Pursuit of Happiness"

In 1776, Jefferson, at thirty-three one of the youngest men at the Continental Congress in Philadelphia, was chosen to write the Declaration of Independence, with the help of John Adams, Benjamin Franklin, and others. The declaration announced that the new United States of America was free from the rule of the British king George III. It has become one of the most famous documents in history. "We hold these truths to be **self-evident**," the declaration states, "that all men are created equal" and that they are born with rights, including "Life, Liberty and the pursuit of Happiness."

History's Greatest Bargain

In 1803, France offered to sell its vast Louisiana **Territory** to the United States for about $15 million. The land would double the size of the country and give the United States control of the entire Mississippi River, which would make it easier for western farmers to ship their goods. Jefferson bought the land, even though the Constitution didn't really give him the right to do so.

In this famous painting of the signing of the Declaration of Independence, Jefferson stands near the center, wearing a red vest.

For forty years, Jefferson worked on his Virginia home, which he called Monticello.

End of a Friendship

When John Adams helped Jefferson write the Declaration of Independence, the two patriots became good friends. In 1796, however, they ran against each other in the election of the country's second president. Adams won, but Jefferson defeated Adams in the next election, in 1800, and became the third president. Adams was bitter about that loss, but in later years, he and Jefferson became friendly again. Both presidents died on July 4, 1826—exactly fifty years after the signing of the Declaration of Independence. Adams's last words were, "Jefferson still survives." What he didn't know was that Jefferson had died just hours earlier.

Acting Against Slavery

As president, Jefferson worked to put an end to the slave trade. He was able to convince the U.S. Congress to pass a law that made it illegal to bring slaves into the United States beginning in 1808. But the law didn't help slaves already here.

SMITHSONIAN LINK
See the desk Jefferson designed and used to write the Declaration of Independence.
http://historywired.si.edu/object.cfm?ID=544

21

James Madison
4TH PRESIDENT
1809–1817

BORN IN VIRGINIA IN 1751;
DIED IN 1836

When the American colonies became the United States of America, a young man named James Madison helped write many of the new country's laws. He also worked on the **Bill of Rights**, the part of the Constitution that guarantees Americans the freedom to say what they want, pray how they want, and write what they want. Almost thirty years later, the "Father of the Constitution" became president.

Small Man, Big Win

James Madison was the smallest man ever elected president—just 5 feet 4 inches tall and only around 100 pounds. Madison served as Thomas Jefferson's secretary of state for eight years, and Jefferson urged Madison to try to follow him as president. The "Great Little Madison" easily won the 1808 election.

Battling Britain

As president, Madison was tested by a conflict with Great Britain. At the time, the United States had good relations with France, and France was at war with Great Britain. When the British began attacking American ships, the United States went to war with them. The War of 1812 began in June 1812 and lasted two and a half years, until the two countries signed a peace treaty. They never fought each other again.

First Lady Saves Washington

In August 1814, British troops attacked Washington, D.C., and burned many buildings, including the president's house. As First Lady Dolley Madison escaped, she rescued such items as the Declaration of Independence and a famous painting of George Washington.

James Monroe
5TH PRESIDENT
1817–1825

BORN IN VIRGINIA IN 1758;
DIED IN 1831

In 1803, President Thomas Jefferson sent James Monroe to France to help make the deal to buy the vast Louisiana Territory. The United States' purchase of the land doubled the size of the country. Fourteen years later, Monroe took charge of the enlarged nation as its president.

Good Feelings

Times were good for most Americans during James Monroe's presidency, and the country was at peace. His years in office became known as the "**Era** of Good Feelings." When Monroe was reelected in 1820, no one ran against him. There were good feelings in the White House, too. The building hosted its first wedding in 1820, when Monroe's daughter Maria married one of her father's assistants.

Hands Off the Americas

In 1823, Monroe declared that the United States would never allow a European country to set up new colonies anywhere in North or South America. This important idea became known as the Monroe Doctrine. The president wanted to let the old powers of Europe know that the United States and the other independent nations of North and South America were ready to defend their side of the Atlantic Ocean.

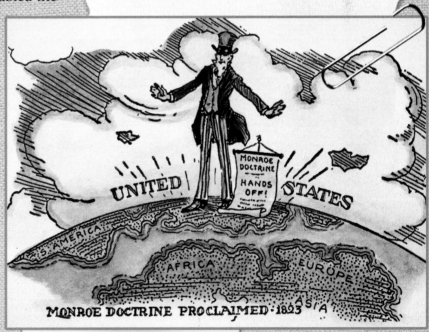

MONROE DOCTRINE PROCLAIMED · 1823

In this cartoon about the Monroe Doctrine, Uncle Sam stands on the Americas and tells the world, "Hands Off!"

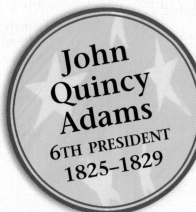

John Quincy Adams
6TH PRESIDENT
1825–1829

***BORN IN MASSACHUSETTS IN 1767;
DIED IN 1848***

As a young man, John Quincy Adams spent much of his time in Europe. Sometimes he traveled with his father, John, who was an important diplomat and later the president. John Quincy also visited England and Russia and was the U.S. ambassador to France from 1809 to 1817. In London, in 1797, Adams met his future wife, Louisa Johnson. She was the only First Lady born outside the United States.

Elected by an Act of Congress

In the election of 1824, Andrew Jackson received more votes than Adams, but neither man won enough electoral votes to become president. As a result, the election had to be settled by the House of Representatives, whose members chose Adams.

A Plan to Build

As president, Adams wanted to spend more tax dollars on roads, railroads, canals, and scientific exploration. But he was not a very popular president. Many Americans were suspicious of his election by Congress; and many members of Congress, who did not want the national government to grow too large, opposed his programs.

In his last moments before dying in the U.S. Capitol, Adams said, "I am content."

Death in the House

After his presidency, Adams was elected to Congress in 1830 and became a powerful leader there. He spoke out against slavery and in favor of a national museum, which would become known as the Smithsonian Institution. In 1848, at the age of eighty, Adams suffered a stroke in the House of Representatives. Too weak to be moved elsewhere, he died in the Capitol two days later.

BORN IN SOUTH CAROLINA IN 1767; DIED IN 1845

Andrew Jackson was the first war hero since Washington to become president. As a general during the War of 1812, he became famous for defeating the British in the Battle of New Orleans. People called him the "Hero of New Orleans," or "Old Hickory" (because they thought he was as tough as a hickory tree).

Wild White House Party

President Jackson believed that the White House belonged to all the people and that all Americans should be welcome there. When he opened up the White House for a celebration the night of his **inauguration**, though, crowds of people smashed dishes, stood on the furniture, and fought over the punch. Jackson escaped from the party through a window and spent his first night as president in a hotel.

This drawing shows the crowds gathering at the White House for Jackson's inaugural party.

General Jackson, on horse-back, leads his troops against the British in the Battle of New Orleans.

The Spoils of Victory

After Jackson returned to the White House, one of his first official acts was to fire almost 1,000 of the government's approximately 10,000 workers. He replaced them with his own supporters. This became know as the **spoils system** when a senator who opposed Jackson's actions complained, "To the victor belong the spoils."

The Indian Removal Act

In 1830, Congress passed the Indian Removal Act, which gave presidents the power to force Native Americans off of their lands in the Southeast. Jackson ordered soldiers to move the Cherokee, Seminole, Creek, and other native groups from their homelands to the American West.

Martin Van Buren
8TH PRESIDENT
1837–1841

BORN IN NEW YORK IN 1782; DIED IN 1862

Martin Van Buren was the first native-born American to be elected president. All of the previous presidents were born before the United States became a country, so they began their lives as citizens of Great Britain.

The Trail of Tears

Van Buren had been Andrew Jackson's vice president, and he continued Jackson's policy of forcing Native Americans to move west. For 116 days in 1838 and 1839, U.S. troops forced 15,000 Cherokee people to leave their homeland in Georgia and move to the territory that today is Oklahoma. Along the way, at least 4,000 died from hunger, disease, cold, or exhaustion. Their march became known as the Trail of Tears.

Hard Times

While Van Buren was president, Americans faced difficult times. Banks across the country went out of business. People lost their jobs. Many Americans blamed the president for failing to find a solution to the crisis. When Van Buren ran for a second term in 1840, angry voters refused to reelect him.

A Lonely President

Van Buren lost his wife, Hannah, many years before he won the presidency. She died of tuberculosis in 1819, at the age of thirty-five. The couple had four sons.

Cherokee tribe members travel west on the Trail of Tears in 1838.

BORN IN VIRGINIA IN 1773; DIED IN 1841

William Henry Harrison became a national hero for leading troops into battle against Native American tribes. In 1811, his soldiers defeated the Shawnee and their chief, Tecumseh, in a major battle near the Tippecanoe River in the territory that is now Indiana. When Harrison ran for president with vice-presidential candidate John Tyler, his supporters wanted to remind voters of his biggest victory. His slogan was "Tippecanoe and Tyler Too."

President for a Month

Harrison became president at the age of sixty-eight, and at the time, he was the oldest man who had ever been elected. At his inauguration, he made a two-hour speech outdoors on a cold and rainy day, without a coat. He caught a cold that day that led to pneumonia. His doctors did all they could, but Harrison died on April 4, 1841. He had been president for exactly one month, and was the first president to die in office. Harrison's wife, Anna, was still at home in Ohio when she heard the news. She had not yet left to travel to Washington, D.C.

Voters remembered Harrison's victory over the Shawnee at Tippecanoe when he ran for president.

Harrison caught a cold at his inauguration on March 4, 1841. A month later, he was dead.

Family Ties

Harrison was part of an important political family. His father, Benjamin, signed the Declaration of Independence, and his grandson, also named Benjamin, would become the nation's twenty-third president.

BORN IN VIRGINIA IN 1790;
DIED IN 1862

No president had ever died in office before, so when William Harrison passed away, many people weren't sure if Vice President John Tyler should have all the powers of a president or just carry out Harrison's plans as an "acting" leader. Tyler, however, insisted, "I am the president," and refused even to open letters addressed "Acting President." Later vice presidents in the same situation have followed his example.

The Party's Over

Tyler was a member of the Whig Party but had many disagreements with the party's leaders. For example, he supported slavery although many Whigs did not. When Tyler refused to sign several bills supported by Whig members of Congress, all but one member of his cabinet quit. Later, Tyler was thrown out of the Whig Party altogether, becoming the first president to lead without a party affiliation.

America Takes Shape

Tyler's secretary of state, Daniel Webster, reached an agreement with Great Britain over the border between Maine and the British colonies of Canada. The treaty also set the U.S.-Canadian border from the Atlantic Ocean to the Rocky Mountains, exactly where the countries are separated today.

PRESIDENT TYLER'S PARTY FOR CHILDREN.

The Largest First Family

No president ever had as many children as Tyler, who was the father of fifteen! He and his first wife, Letitia, had eight children. She died of a stroke while Tyler was president. He later became the first president to get married while in office when he wed his second wife, Julia. The couple had seven children of their own.

President Tyler opened the White House to a birthday party for his oldest granddaughter.

James Knox Polk
11TH PRESIDENT
1845–1849

BORN IN NORTH CAROLINA IN 1795;
DIED IN 1849

James Polk promised voters that he would help the United States stretch from the Atlantic Ocean to the Pacific Ocean. This popular idea was known as **manifest destiny**. As president, Polk agreed to a treaty with Great Britain that gave the United States territory that would become Oregon, Washington, Idaho, and parts of Wyoming and Montana. The country now stretched all the way across North America.

War with Mexico

Texas had become a state in 1845, but the United States and Mexico still argued over the state's southern border. Polk offered to buy the land in dispute, as well as the territory that is now California and New Mexico. When Mexico refused to deal, Polk sent troops led by General Zachary Taylor to Texas. In 1846, war broke out. Although Mexico had more soldiers, Taylor's strategies led to victory. In the treaty ending the war, the United States got the territory it wanted.

This 1844 campaign poster supported Polk, left, and his vice president, George Dallas.

A Man of His Word

When he ran for president, Polk promised he would serve only one term. Although he was very popular after the victory over Mexico, he kept his word and did not run again. Polk hoped for a happy retirement. Instead, he became ill and died three months after leaving the White House.

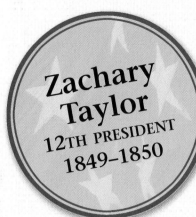

Zachary Taylor
12TH PRESIDENT
1849–1850

BORN IN VIRGINIA IN 1784; DIED IN 1850

After leading U.S. troops to victory over Mexico, Zachary Taylor was a national hero. In 1848, the tough general, nicknamed "Old Rough and Ready," was elected president.

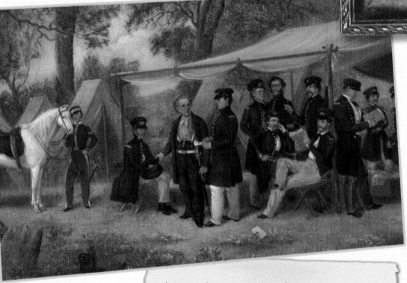

Less than a year after the end of the war with Mexico, General Taylor, center, became president.

The Rush for Gold

In 1848, gold was discovered in the territory of California. As people rushed there hoping to find a fortune, the territory's population grew to more than 100,000. According to the laws of the time, that was more than enough people for California to become a state.

Slaves in the West?

In 1849, slavery had been outlawed in states (mostly Northern). It was allowed in fifteen Southern states. Taylor wanted California to be a free state, without slaves. Southern leaders threatened to **secede**, or leave the country, if that happened. Senator Henry Clay suggested that Congress allow California to become a free state but also pass the Fugitive Slave Act, giving slave owners the right to travel to Northern states and capture escaped slaves.

A Surprise Ending

Taylor hated Clay's idea and said he'd go to war with Southern states if they seceded. Americans wondered if a war between the states would break out. Then, after the July 4 ceremonies in 1850, the president came home to the White House and ate some cherries and milk. One or the other had spoiled, and Taylor became ill. He died five days later.

BORN IN NEW YORK IN 1800; DIED IN 1874

Millard Fillmore was the son of a poor farmer. As a young child, he rarely went to school. When he was nineteen, he asked a twenty-one-year-old teacher, Abigail Powers, to help him learn to read and write. She was an excellent tutor. Fillmore became a wealthy lawyer and, eventually, president. Abigail became his wife and, later, the First Lady.

Shut Out

The Whig Party **nominated** Fillmore as Zachary Taylor's vice president, but Fillmore didn't even meet Taylor until after the election. President Taylor gave him no responsibilities in the government. But when Taylor died, Fillmore took over.

The Compromise of 1850

Taylor had opposed Henry Clay's Compromise of 1850, the bills that would allow California to become a new, free state and also allow Southerners to capture escaped slaves under the Fugitive Slave Act. After Taylor's death, however, Fillmore signed the bills. He thought it was the only way to avoid a war between the North and the South. But Whig Party leaders were furious that Fillmore had allowed the Fugitive Slave Act to become a law. They refused to nominate him for reelection.

Uncle Tom's Cabin

In 1852, Harriet Beecher Stowe wrote a novel about slavery called *Uncle Tom's Cabin*. It became one of the country's most popular books and convinced many Americans that slavery was terrible. Throughout the North, people began refusing to obey the Fugitive Slave Act. Instead, some protected escaped slaves. Slowly but surely, the debate over slavery was dividing the country.

The elderly slave Uncle Tom and the young girl Eva are two of the main characters in *Uncle Tom's Cabin*.

BORN IN NEW HAMPSHIRE IN 1804;
DIED IN 1869

Franklin Pierce left the U.S. Senate in 1842, hoping never to return to Washington, D.C., a city he did not like. But when Democratic Party leaders could not decide on a candidate for the 1852 election, they called on Pierce and he agreed to run. The party's slogan was "We Polked You in 1844. We'll Pierce You in 1852."

A Sad Term

Pierce and his wife, Jane, had three children, all of them sons. All three died before he became president. The Pierces' last son, Benjamin, was killed in a train accident just weeks before his father's inauguration. He was eleven years old.

Land for Sale

Pierce made a deal with Mexico to buy the land that is now the southern part of Arizona and New Mexico. He also tried to buy the island of Cuba from Spain, but antislavery members of Congress voted against it.

Bleeding Kansas

In 1854, Pierce signed the Kansas-Nebraska Act into law. The act divided the Nebraska Territory into two territories, which would become Kansas and Nebraska. Settlers there could decide for themselves whether their new states would allow slavery. Most people in Nebraska opposed slavery, but those in Kansas weren't so sure. Fights between slavery supporters and opponents left more than 200 people dead. The territory became known as Bleeding Kansas. Democrats did not like how Pierce handled the crisis and did not support him for reelection in 1856.

After years of disputes over whether to allow slavery in the territory, Kansas became a free state in 1861.

BORN IN PENNSYLVANIA IN 1791; DIED IN 1868

James Buchanan is the only president who never got married. His niece, Harriet Lane, acted as First Lady and was the hostess for parties, including one for England's Prince of Wales. More than ninety years after the American Revolution, the prince was the first British royal to stay in the White House.

An Election and a Walkout

The antislavery Republican Party nominated Abraham Lincoln for president in 1860. Southern states threatened to secede if he won. Lincoln had said, "A house divided against itself cannot stand." He was right. Between his election and his inauguration, seven Southern states seceded and formed the Confederate States of America. Buchanan thought secession was illegal, but he did not want a war, and so he did little to try to stop the states from leaving. The United States had finally split in two.

Citizens or Property?

Buchanan told Americans that they didn't need to have a debate over slavery. Since the Constitution allowed slavery, it was legal wherever states permitted it—and that was the end of the matter, as far as he was concerned. The Supreme Court agreed that slavery was legal. In 1857, it ruled that an escaped slave, Dred Scott, could not sue for the right to be free because slaves were property, not citizens, no matter what state they happened to live in. Americans who opposed slavery were outraged.

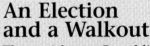

NOW READY:
THE
Dred Scott Decision.
OPINION OF CHIEF-JUSTICE
ROGER B. TANEY,
WITH AN INTRODUCTION,
BY DR. J. H. VAN EVRIE.
ALSO,
AN APPENDIX,
BY SAM. A. CARTWRIGHT, M.D., of New Orleans,
ENTITLED,
"Natural History of the Prognathous
Race of Mankind."
ORIGINALLY WRITTEN FOR THE NEW YORK DAY-BOOK.

THE GREAT WANT OF A BRIEF PAMPHLET, containing the famous decision of Chief-Justice Taney, in the celebrated Dred Scott Case, has induced the Publishers of the DAY-BOOK to present this edition to the public. It contains a Historical Introduction by Dr. Van Evrie, author of "Negroes and Negro Slavery," and an Appendix

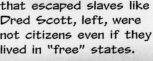

The Supreme Court ruled that escaped slaves like Dred Scott, left, were not citizens even if they lived in "free" states.

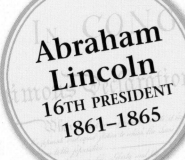

Abraham Lincoln
16TH PRESIDENT
1861–1865

*BORN IN KENTUCKY IN 1809;
DIED IN 1865*

Abraham Lincoln was born to a poor family in Kentucky and attended school for less than one year. As a young man, he worked as a wood splitter, a ferry captain, and a postmaster. But he read constantly. One of his favorite books was Parson Weems's famous biography of George Washington, which was full of stories (not all true) about the first president. Lincoln also taught himself the law and became one of Illinois's most successful lawyers.

Great Debates

In 1858, Lincoln ran for U.S. senator from Illinois against Stephen Douglas. The two men had a series of debates that made them both famous nationwide. Douglas won the Senate race, but two years later, Lincoln would be elected president.

The Civil War Begins

Lincoln had been in office only six weeks when the Civil War began, with a Confederate attack on South Carolina's Fort Sumter on April 12, 1861. The war would last four years, and more than 600,000 Americans would die fighting in it—more than in all other U.S. wars combined. The North, or the Union, had more money, supplies, and soldiers than the South, or Confederacy. But

Lincoln had a hard time finding a general who could lead the Union to victory. Several men were given the job and then fired when they could not produce victories. Finally, Ulysses S. Grant took command in 1864 and began winning major battles.

Freeing the Slaves

Lincoln once said, "Whenever I hear anyone arguing for slavery, I feel a strong impulse to see it tried on him personally." Still, at the start of the war, Lincoln said it was more important to keep the country together than to end slavery. But in 1863, the president did just that. He issued the Emancipation Proclamation, which freed all slaves living in the Confederate states. Eventually, 200,000 free African Americans fought in the Union army and navy. After the war, they would remain free, Lincoln said, because "the promise, being made, must be kept."

The Gettysburg Address has only 269 words, but many believe it is one of the greatest speeches in U.S. history.

The Gettysburg Address

The 1863 Battle of Gettysburg, in Pennsylvania, was the bloodiest battle in the war, with more than 50,000 casualties. But the Union victory was a turning point. Four months after the battle, Lincoln traveled to Gettysburg to speak at the opening of a cemetery for soldiers who had died there. In his famous short speech, now known as the Gettysburg Address, Lincoln told Americans they had to win the war to make sure "that government of the people, by the people, for the people shall not perish from the earth." In his speech, Lincoln said, "The world will little note nor long remember what we say here." He was never more wrong, nor more humble.

35

Abraham Lincoln

End of the War

In 1864, with the Union close to victory in the war, Lincoln was elected to a second term, defeating George McClellan, one of the generals he had fired. In his second inaugural speech, Lincoln said he planned to reunite the nation after the war "with charity for all." Lincoln did not want to punish Southerners, he said, but to bring them back into the Union without "malice," or ill feelings. He never got the chance. The war ended with the Confederacy's surrender on April 9, 1865, but Lincoln died just days later.

First Lady in Mourning

Mary Todd Lincoln was in many ways the opposite of her husband. He was tall and skinny; she was short and heavy. He grew up poor and educated himself, while she was a wealthy girl who had a fine formal education. Despite their differences, the Lincolns were devoted to each other. Their life together was not always happy, however. The Lincolns had four sons, but three died young. William, who was eleven, died in the White House in 1862. His loss crushed the First Lady. Then, after her husband's death, she fell into a depression, which she never got over. Eventually she needed to be treated for mental illness.

Death of a President

Today, Lincoln may be the most admired president in history, but while he was in office he received many threatening letters from people who wanted to kill him. Yet Lincoln said, "I cannot bring myself to believe that any human being lives who would do me any harm." Then, on April 14, 1865, while the president and his wife, Mary, attended a play in Washington, a treasonous actor, John Wilkes Booth, shot and killed him. The challenge of reuniting America now belonged to the new president, Andrew Johnson.

John Wilkes Booth shot Lincoln in the back of the head while the president sat in this chair in Ford's Theatre.

SMITHSONIAN LINK
Visit an online exhibit about Lincoln's life, including campaign posters, cartoons, and the top hat he wore on the night he was assassinated.
http://civilwar.si.edu/lincoln_intro.html

Andrew Johnson
17TH PRESIDENT
1865–1869

BORN IN NORTH CAROLINA IN 1808; DIED IN 1875

Andrew Johnson's father died when he was three, and his family was very poor. He never went to school, and his wife, Eliza, later taught him how to read and write. At age twelve, Johnson began working for a tailor. He never forgot the skills he learned. Even as president, Johnson made his own suits.

Loyal to the Union

When the Civil War began, Johnson, then a U.S. senator from Tennessee, was the only Southern senator who remained loyal to the Union. To reward Johnson, Lincoln made him his vice-presidential candidate in the election of 1864. Johnson had been in office only forty-one days when Lincoln died.

A President on Trial

Members of Congress were so angry about Johnson's policies that in 1868 they tried to **impeach** him, or remove him from office. The House of Representatives voted to impeach Johnson, but the Senate failed to— by just one vote.

In this drawing, Johnson is ordered to appear in Congress for his impeachment trial. Visitors could not get into the trial without a ticket.

After the War

Johnson was faced with huge challenges, such as reuniting the country and helping former slaves find work. Johnson had supported the Union during the war, but he agreed with other Southerners that former slaves should not be allowed to become American citizens. Congress disagreed, and in 1865, voted to amend the Constitution to make African Americans citizens. On issue after issue, Johnson vetoed bills that would force Southern states to give rights to African Americans. Time after time, Congress voted to override his veto.

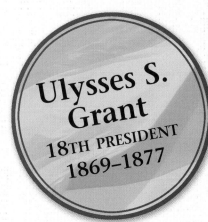

Ulysses S. Grant
18TH PRESIDENT
1869–1877

BORN IN OHIO IN 1822; DIED IN 1885

As the general in charge of the Union army, Ulysses S. Grant helped the North win the Civil War. He was an unlikely hero. Grant had left the army in 1854 as a captain, after eleven years of service. He failed in several tries to run a business. Then Union army leaders, short of experienced officers at the start of the war, asked him to return as a colonel. He quickly rose to the rank of general. Lincoln liked how Grant led his troops. "I can't spare this man," Lincoln said. "He fights." But in private, Grant was a gentle man who hated the sight of blood.

Scandal After Scandal

Grant was a great general and an honest man, but he had no experience in politics. Several times during his two terms as president, men he had hired for important government jobs turned out to be untrustworthy. Scandals over bribes, stolen taxes, and other crimes made it difficult for Grant to lead the country.

Two Is Enough

Despite the problems of his presidency, Grant himself remained popular. In fact, many people thought he should run for a third term. No president had ever done that, and Grant decided not to become the first. Once he left the White House, he wrote a book about his life, finishing it just three days before he died. It became a bestseller.

General U. S. Grant (front, center) got the nickname "Unconditional Surrender" Grant because of his many Civil War victories.

SMITHSONIAN LINK
See a picture of General Grant taken by famous Civil War photographer Mathew Brady and learn of Brady's secret reason for visiting the general.
www.npg.si.edu/exh/brady/gallery/56gal.html

BORN IN OHIO IN 1822; DIED IN 1893

Rutherford Hayes and his wife, Lucy, were introduced to each other by their mothers, who were good friends. Lucy was the first college graduate to become First Lady. The couple had eight children, although three died before Hayes became president. They also hosted the first White House Easter Egg Roll, in 1878. It's an annual tradition that continues today.

President or Fraud?

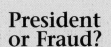

In the election of 1876, Democrat Samuel Tilden of New York received more votes than the Republican candidate, Hayes. But the electoral votes of three states were disputed. A special **commission** made up of congressmen and Supreme Court justices and led by Republicans decided the election for Hayes, by one electoral vote. Furious Democrats called the new president "Rutherfraud Hayes."

Calling the President

Hayes was the first president who had a telephone installed in the White House. His number was easy to remember: 1.

A Difficult Deal

In a compromise with Democrats after the election, Hayes agreed to remove the U.S. troops who had been stationed in the former Confederate states since the end of the Civil War. Once the soldiers left, many Southern leaders began to change or ignore laws that had given equal rights to African Americans. For many years after, it was difficult for African Americans in the South to vote or to attend good schools.

After the Civil War, many African Americans attended freedmen's schools in the South like this one.

BORN IN NEW JERSEY IN 1831;
DIED IN 1881

Rutherford Hayes decided not to seek reelection in 1880. Instead, the leading Republican candidate appeared to be former president Ulysses S. Grant. Grant had changed his mind and decided to try to become the first person elected president three times. But Grant did not have quite enough support at his party's convention. After thirty-six votes, party leaders settled on a different candidate: Representative James Garfield of Ohio. He defeated Democrat Winfield Hancock to win the election.

Spoiling the System

Since the days of Andrew Jackson, presidents and their parties had followed the spoils system, handing important government jobs to their friends and political supporters. Garfield wanted to limit the spoils system and give more jobs to the best-qualified people. In a showdown with fellow Republicans in Congress, he succeeded in naming his own candidates to some key jobs.

SMITHSONIAN LINK
Learn more about the assassination of Garfield and see the device that telephone inventor Alexander Graham Bell used to try to save the president's life.
http://americanhistory.si.edu/presidency/3d1d.html

A President Murdered

Garfield won the battle in Congress to cut back the spoils system, but the issue would cost him his life. On July 2, 1881, a New York Republican who had hoped to be given a government job for his work in the election shot Garfield in a Washington train station. For several weeks doctors tried to save the president, but one of them probably infected Garfield's wound with his dirty hands. Garfield died of blood poisoning.

After Garfield was shot, doctors treated him in the White House, then moved him to New Jersey to get away from the summer heat. They still could not save him.

BORN IN VERMONT IN 1830; DIED IN 1886

Chester Arthur moved to New York in 1854 and became a leading lawyer, often taking cases for African Americans. In one famous case, he sued a New York railroad company for refusing to let a black woman, Lizzie Jennings, sit in a "whites-only" car. Arthur won the case, which ended racial separation on New York City trains.

Looking Good, Feeling Bad

Arthur was known for his good taste. He owned eighty pairs of pants and redecorated the White House in the latest styles. However, Arthur lived with great sadness. His wife, Ellen, had died just before he was elected to his own term as president. Also, though the president told few people, he knew he was very ill with kidney disease. He died a year after leaving office.

The Best Person for the Job

Garfield had wanted to do away with the spoils system. But after his death, hardly anyone expected Arthur to continue Garfield's plans. Arthur's whole political career had been based on helping his party, and on giving and receiving political favors. He had been chosen as vice president only to win the support of New York Republicans. So the country was shocked when Arthur went even further than Garfield to change the political system. One major step was signing the Pendleton Act, which required people to pass **civil service** tests before they could get government jobs.

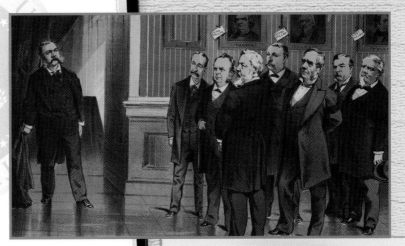

The title of this print made before Arthur's inauguration summed up the feelings of many Americans: "What have we to expect of him?"

BORN IN NEW JERSEY IN 1837; DIED IN 1908

Since Abraham Lincoln was elected in 1860, the Republican Party had won every race for the White House. In the 1884 election, Democrats were eager for a victory. Their candidate, Governor Grover Cleveland of New York, was known for standing up to corrupt politicians, which made him popular with voters. He defeated James Blaine and became president.

Fair Prices

Railroads were one of the nation's biggest businesses, but there were few laws about how much the railroad companies could charge for letting people travel on trains or ship products by rail. Some railroad companies charged outrageous prices, and Congress wanted to put an end to that. Cleveland agreed. He signed the Interstate Commerce Act, which required railroad companies to charge "reasonable and just" prices, and set up a government **agency** to make sure they did.

SMITHSONIAN LINK
See the dress Frances Folsom wore when she married Grover Cleveland in the White House.
http://historywired.si.edu/object.cfm?ID=316

A White House Wedding

Cleveland became the first president to get married in the White House when he wed twenty-one-year-old Frances Folsom in the building's Blue Room in 1886. Folsom, the daughter of Cleveland's former law partner, was the youngest person ever to become First Lady. She called her forty-nine-year-old husband "Uncle Cleve." After Cleveland lost the 1888 election to Benjamin Harrison, Frances predicted that her family would return to the White House. She was right.

Frances Folsom Cleveland became the only First Lady to give birth inside the White House when her second child, Esther, was born in 1893.

BORN IN OHIO IN 1833; DIED IN 1901

Benjamin Harrison's great-grandfather signed the Declaration of Independence. His grandfather was the ninth president, and his father was elected to Congress. When Harrison ran for president in 1888, his Democratic opponents teased him by calling him "Little Ben," because he was only 5 feet 6 inches tall. To answer them, the Republican's slogan was "Grandfather's Hat Fits!"

Fighting Big Business

Oil companies were buying other oil companies, and becoming bigger and bigger. Railroads were doing the same. Americans worried that these combined companies, or **trusts**, could charge consumers high prices because they would have no competition. Harrison signed the Sherman Antitrust Act in 1890. It was meant to protect Americans from unfair prices when a single company tried to buy its competitors and corner, or take over, an entire industry.

Disaster at Wounded Knee

During Harrison's term, ugly battles continued between Native Americans and U.S. troops in the West. Late in 1890, the American Seventh Cavalry killed more than 200 Sioux near Wounded Knee Creek, in South Dakota. The Sioux had surrendered to the troops the day before; but when a fight broke out with one Sioux man, the troops fired into a crowd, killing men, women, and children.

After the killings at Wounded Knee, soldiers buried many of the Sioux victims in a mass grave.

BORN IN NEW JERSEY IN 1837; DIED IN 1908

The 1892 election was a rematch between Benjamin Harrison and former president Grover Cleveland. Although their first race had been close, this one wasn't. Cleveland won by almost 400,000 votes, and became the only president ever to be elected to two terms that weren't consecutive, or following one after the other.

Top-Secret Surgery

In 1893, doctors discovered a cancerous tumor in the president's mouth. He would need surgery to remove it. But Cleveland did not want Americans to know he was ill while he was dealing with the Panic of 1893. Instead, he had the surgery done in secret, on a boat in New York City's East River. Doctors replaced part of the president's jaw, but none of them talked about the surgery until 1917.

A National Crisis

The country's economy weakened greatly during Cleveland's second term. The Panic of 1893 caused many businesses to fail, including some railroads. Thousands of Americans lost their jobs. Other workers were angry that companies cut their pay. In 1894, to protest pay cuts, 120,000 railroad workers went on strike in Chicago, Illinois. They blocked railroad tracks and kept many trains from traveling to the West, so Cleveland sent U.S. troops to break up the strike. This angered many Americans, who believed that the government should support workers, not companies.

Soldiers on horseback guarded the first trains leaving Chicago after the railroad strike.

44

BORN IN OHIO IN 1843; DIED IN 1901

When William McKinley was a lieutenant during the Civil War, his commander was Rutherford Hayes. The two future presidents became friends, and after the war, McKinley helped Hayes campaign for governor of Ohio.

"A Splendid Little War"

Cuba, an island not far from Florida, was a Spanish colony in 1895 when Cubans began a revolt against Spain. Many Americans wanted to go to war with Spain after reading newspaper reports (which may not have been true) about the Spanish torturing Cubans. McKinley tried to avoid a battle with Spain, but when the U.S. battleship *Maine* sank after an explosion off Cuba's coast in 1898, he declared war. His secretary of state called the Spanish-American War, which the U.S. won in just 100 days, a "splendid little war," although several thousand American soldiers died in battle or from disease. After the war, Cuba became independent, and the U.S. took control of the Spanish territories of Puerto Rico, Guam, and the Philippines.

The U.S. accused Spain of blowing up the *Maine* with a mine, but Spanish officials said the explosion that sank the ship took place onboard.

SMITHSONIAN LINK
Learn more about the Spanish-American War and see the sunken battleship *Maine*.
http://americanhistory.si.edu/militaryhistory/printable/section.asp?id=7

A Short Second Term

McKinley was reelected easily in 1900. But just a few months into his second term, he was shot by an unemployed worker in Buffalo, New York. As soldiers took the shooter away, McKinley told them not to hurt the man. The president died eight days later. After his murder, the agents of the government's Secret Service began guarding presidents, as they still do today.

Theodore Roosevelt
26TH PRESIDENT
1901–1909

***BORN IN NEW YORK IN 1858;
DIED IN 1919***

As a child, Theodore Roosevelt was a sickly boy who suffered from asthma. But he became stronger as he grew up. Years later, after the death of his first wife, Alice, he spent two years in the Dakota Territory, where he hunted, rode horses, hiked, and gained a love of the outdoors. As president, he helped to protect millions of acres of forests and create five national parks.

The Trust Buster

Like Benjamin Harrison, Roosevelt worked with Congress to make laws to limit the power of trusts, large companies that bought their competitors and set unfairly high prices. He also helped workers who went on strike. At the time, large companies often hired private security guards to try to break up strikes, sometimes violently. When a group of coal miners went on strike in Pennsylvania in 1902, the president sent troops to the area to protect workers until a fair agreement could be reached.

America's Favorite Family

Roosevelt's six children became well known for their wild antics in the White House. His two youngest sons would slide down the main staircase on metal trays, and one of them once rode a pony up the stairs. The president often left his office at four o'clock in the afternoon to play with his "blessed bunnies."

In 1904, voters decided to give the family four more years in the White House: after completing McKinley's term, Roosevelt was elected by a huge majority.

Teddy Bear

On a hunting trip to Mississippi in 1902, Roosevelt's dogs trapped a bear, but when the president saw it was only a cub, he refused to shoot it. The story spread across the country, and toy makers soon began selling stuffed "Teddy's bears," now known as teddy bears.

Man of Peace

In 1904, war broke out between Russia and Japan. Although the war did not involve the United States, Roosevelt helped the two countries reach a peace agreement. When they signed their treaty in 1905, leaders of both nations gave the president credit for helping to end their war.

SMITHSONIAN LINK
Visit an exhibit about the life of Theodore Roosevelt, including pictures of one of the first teddy bears and his daughter's White House wedding.
www.npg.si.edu/exh/roosevelt/rrwh2.htm

Roosevelt gave up his job as assistant secretary of the navy to lead the Rough Riders into battle in Cuba.

Rough Rider

Roosevelt became a national hero during the Spanish-American War when he led a group of volunteer fighters, nicknamed the "Rough Riders," to victory in a key battle in Cuba. Later that year, he was elected governor of New York. Two years later, he was vice president. After McKinley's death, the Rough Rider, only forty-two years old, became the country's youngest president yet.

Couldn't Stay Away

During the 1904 campaign, Roosevelt promised he would not run for reelection in 1908. Although he had changed his mind by then, he kept his word and stayed out of the race. Instead, he urged voters to support William Howard Taft. But in 1912, Roosevelt did run for president again, as the candidate of the Progressive Party. He finished second, ahead of Taft but behind Woodrow Wilson.

William Howard Taft

27TH PRESIDENT
1909–1913

BORN IN OHIO IN 1857;
DIED IN 1930

William Howard Taft, the heaviest president ever, weighed more than 300 pounds when he was elected. He had to have a new, larger bathtub put in the White House after he got stuck in the old one. But he was also athletic. He played golf often, and loved baseball, although he was a better hitter than runner.

Dreaming of Washington

Helen Taft had always wanted to be First Lady, and she encouraged William to take jobs that might help him become president. For example, he became governor of the territory of the Philippines after the Spanish-American War. After her husband was elected, she had the first cherry trees planted in Washington. They continue to bloom in the capital each spring.

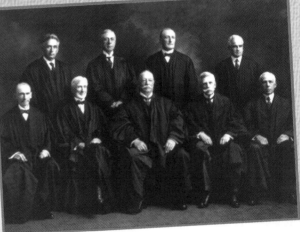

As chief justice, Taft, sitting at center, tried to keep his weight down by walking three miles from his home to the Supreme Court building, and back, almost every day.

Hard Act to Follow

Taft accomplished a lot as president. He turned nearly as much American land into national parks as Roosevelt had, and took action against twice as many trusts. But he was criticized whenever he did something different from Roosevelt. Early in Taft's term, former president Roosevelt took a trip to Africa, which got as much attention as anything the new president did. By 1910, the two men were no longer friends.

Dream Job

Taft once said, "Politics . . . makes me sick." He preferred being a judge. Ten years after Taft lost the election of 1912, President Warren Harding named him chief justice of the Supreme Court. Taft is the only man ever to hold both jobs. He was so happy on the Court that he wrote, "I don't remember that I ever was president."

48

BORN IN VIRGINIA IN 1856; DIED IN 1924

As a child, Woodrow Wilson had trouble reading. But he went on to become a great scholar and the president of Princeton University, in New Jersey. Wilson studied political science, and Democratic leaders convinced him to leave the university and practice what he had learned, first as governor of New Jersey and later as president.

World War I

In 1914, old conflicts in Europe finally led to war. Germany, Austria-Hungary, and the Ottoman Empire, on one side, fought France, the United Kingdom, Italy, and Russia on the other. Wilson didn't want the United States to get involved in World War I. In fact, when he ran for reelection in 1916, one of his slogans was "He Kept Us Out of War." But soon after the Germans tried to convince Mexico to join the fight against the United States, Wilson declared war against Germany. The president said that Americans would fight to make the world "safe for democracy," and that he hoped it would be the war to end all wars. The United States sent more than a million troops to Europe and helped its allies win.

In Paris, the president was given a hero's welcome after World War I.

The White House Pitches In

During the war, Americans were told to ration, or limit, their use of important resources such as food and oil. The Wilsons did their part. They used no gas on Sundays, and ate no meat on Mondays and no wheat on Tuesdays. They also kept a flock of sheep on the White House lawn, so the grass never had to be mowed. Wool from the sheep was used to make blankets for the army.

Woodrow Wilson

American cartoons wondered whether Wilson would be able to help give birth to the League of Nations.

Out of His League

Wilson helped negotiate the treaty that ended World War I. It included plans for a new worldwide organization, the League of Nations, meant to help countries avoid wars in the future. The Senate, however, debated about joining the League, then voted to keep the United States out of it. An angry Wilson set out to tour the country and urge people to tell their senators to support the League. Three weeks into his tour, he suffered a severe stroke.

Who's in Charge?

Wilson's first wife, Ellen, had died in 1914 of kidney disease. To the surprise of many Americans, Wilson remarried a year later. After Wilson's stroke in 1919, the president was rarely seen in public. His new wife, Edith, above, helped to nurse him; but many Americans, including members of Congress, wondered if she was actually running the country in her husband's place. Historians continue to debate who was really in charge during Wilson's last days in the White House.

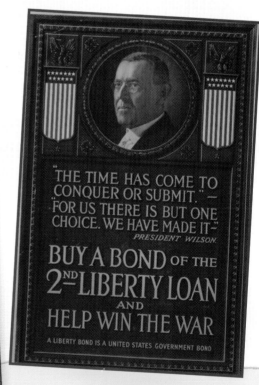

"THE TIME HAS COME TO CONQUER OR SUBMIT." — FOR US THERE IS BUT ONE CHOICE. WE HAVE MADE IT.—
PRESIDENT WILSON.

BUY A BOND OF THE 2ND LIBERTY LOAN AND HELP WIN THE WAR

A LIBERTY BOND IS A UNITED STATES GOVERNMENT BOND

Wilson asked Americans to support the war by buying special war bonds, which was a way of loaning money to the government.

BORN IN OHIO IN 1865; DIED IN 1923

Warren Harding was the first president elected in part by women. The Nineteenth Amendment to the Constitution became law in 1920, giving women the right to vote (also known as suffrage). Harding's wife, Florence, was a major supporter of women's suffrage. She helped to manage her husband's presidential campaign too.

White House Scandals

Harding brought several close friends to Washington to take jobs in his cabinet or work as advisers. The president often played poker with his friends. In one famous game he gambled and lost a set of the White House's dishes. There was a more serious scandal ahead, though: Harding's secretary of the interior, who was in charge of the government's land, took a $300,000 bribe to rent public land in Teapot Dome, Wyoming, to the Mammoth Oil Company. The Teapot Dome scandal might have ruined Harding's term, but it was not discovered until after the president died of a heart attack in 1923, while on a railroad tour of the country. Vice President Calvin Coolidge would have to deal with the scandal instead.

American women were kept out of thirty-three presidential elections before voters like these in New York City could cast their ballots in 1920.

Closing the Door

During the early 1900s, hundreds of thousands of immigrants came to America from eastern and southern Europe. The newcomers were needed. There were more jobs on farms and in factories than there were workers to fill them, but some Americans feared that the new arrivals might work for less money and take their jobs away. Harding agreed, and he signed a bill in 1921 that set limits on immigration to the United States for the first time in the country's history.

Harding brought so many friends from his home state to work in the White House, they became known as "the Ohio gang."

Calvin Coolidge
30TH PRESIDENT
1923–1929

BORN IN VERMONT IN 1872;
DIED IN 1933

As the scandals of Harding's term became public, new president Calvin Coolidge stayed calm. He took strong action to uncover corruption and restore people's faith in the government. In 1924, Republicans urged voters to "Keep Cool with Coolidge," and the former Massachusetts governor, nicknamed "Silent Cal," was elected to a full term in office.

Hands Off

Coolidge often said, "The business of America is business." He was convinced that if the government stayed out of the way, businesses would grow and all Americans would benefit from new job opportunities. Coolidge successfully urged Congress to cut taxes, and he supported other policies to help businesses. More Americans began investing their money in the stock market, hoping to share in the businesses' profits. During Coolidge's term, the economy boomed and people celebrated the Roaring Twenties. But in 1929, when the economy took a major downturn, those stock investments would leave many families broke.

Helen Keller, right, used her hands to read Mrs. Coolidge's lips.

The First Lady of Sign Language

While President Coolidge could be quiet and shy, his wife, Grace, was cheerful and sociable. When she met Coolidge, she was a teacher at a school for the deaf. As First Lady, she gave a speech entirely in sign language and met with the famous writer Helen Keller, who was both deaf and blind.

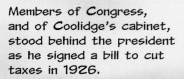

Members of Congress, and of Coolidge's cabinet, stood behind the president as he signed a bill to cut taxes in 1926.

BORN IN IOWA IN 1874; DIED IN 1964

Herbert Hoover and his wife, Lou, met as geology students at Stanford University in California. Hoover became an engineer, and the young couple traveled the world managing mines. In China they learned to speak Chinese, a skill they used in the White House when they didn't want people to know what they were saying to each other.

Poverty Fighter

Hoover became a hero for running programs that delivered food and supplies to people starving in Europe during World War I. When he ran for president, he promised "a triumph over poverty" and "a chicken in every pot." It would quickly become impossible for Hoover to keep those promises.

The Great Depression

In the 1920s, many Americans invested their savings in companies through the stock market. But on October 29, 1929, or "Black Tuesday," the value of many stocks dropped. This crash caused people to lose billions of dollars. Soon, 5,000 banks went out of business, leaving nine million people broke. In the months ahead, about 100,000 people lost their jobs each week. Families had to give up their homes and farms, and thousands went hungry.

As the Depression wiped out people's savings, men like this New Yorker tried to sell whatever they could, even their cars.

Thousands of people lost their homes and moved into Hooverville shacks in cities across the country.

Living in Hooverville

Hoover tried hard, but he could not end the Great Depression. He did not want the government to give money directly to unemployed workers. He thought that was un-American. Poor Americans began to resent Hoover. Homeless people called their shacks "Hoovervilles." The newspapers they used to keep warm were "Hoover blankets," and the rabbits they killed for food were "Hoover hogs."

53

Franklin D. Roosevelt
32ND PRESIDENT
1933–1945

BORN IN NEW YORK IN 1882;
DIED IN 1945

Franklin D. Roosevelt followed his distant cousin Theodore into government and was the losing vice-presidential candidate in 1920. A year later, at age thirty-nine, he was struck by polio, a disease that left his legs paralyzed. For the rest of his life, Roosevelt would rely on leg braces and wheelchairs. But by 1928, he felt strong enough to return to politics, and New Yorkers elected him governor.

The New Deal

After defeating Hoover in the 1932 election, Roosevelt told Americans, "The only thing we have to fear is fear itself," and promised "action, and action now." Roosevelt took drastic steps to help get the country out of the Great Depression. Working with Congress, he launched a series of programs he called the New Deal. As part of the plan, the government put millions of unemployed Americans to work building roads, schools, and dams. The new Social Security program promised government payments to people who were elderly, unemployed, or disabled. The New Deal was expensive, and the government had never tried anything like it before; but it did get Americans working again.

Order in the Court

Roosevelt's fellow Democrats in Congress supported his New Deal programs, but the Supreme Court ruled that some parts of his plan went against the Constitution, because the president was using powers that belonged to Congress or the states. In 1937, Roosevelt proposed adding six more justices to the Court. Since Roosevelt would have been able to choose the judges, they would probably have agreed with his plans. While many Americans supported the New Deal, the idea of changing the Supreme Court's structure just to help Roosevelt worried them. The Senate rejected the plan.

After the Pearl Harbor attack, Roosevelt told Americans that fighting in World War II would be "the most tremendous undertaking of our American history."

World War II

World War II began in Europe in 1939. Under the rule of Adolf Hitler and his Nazi Party, Germany conquered several of its neighbors, including France. By June 1940, Great Britain stood alone against Germany. Roosevelt said that he did not want the United States to enter the war, but that the country had to try to help its ally. Although many Americans disagreed, the president and Congress sent warships and weapons to Great Britain. The government also began **drafting** Americans into the army, even though the country was not yet at war. That changed on December 7, 1941, when Japanese planes launched a surprise attack on the U.S. naval base at Pearl Harbor, Hawaii. Japan was an ally of Germany, and Roosevelt and Congress quickly declared war on both countries. Soon millions of Americans joined the military, and factories began producing guns, tanks, and planes twenty-four hours a day. The president also decided to spend $2 billion on a secret project to build an atomic bomb. The idea was suggested to him by the world's most famous scientist, Albert Einstein, who thought the Germans were already trying to build an atomic bomb. "We are now in this war," Roosevelt said. "We are all in it all the way."

Franklin D. Roosevelt

Japanese Internment

Many Japanese Americans lived on America's West Coast in the 1940s. After Pearl Harbor, some Americans worried that these citizens and immigrants might become spies for Japan. In February 1942, Roosevelt ordered 127,000 Japanese Americans to move to **internment camps** far from their homes on the West Coast. Although Germany and Italy also fought against the United States, only Japanese Americans were sent to the camps. Years later the government apologized to the families.

President for Life?

Following George Washington's example, no president had ever campaigned for a third term. Roosevelt had been reelected easily in 1936. In 1940, he wanted to stay in office but did not want to break with tradition by saying he wanted to run again. Instead, Democrats asked Roosevelt to be their nominee in 1940. He agreed, and was elected for a third time. In 1951, the Constitution was changed to set a limit of two elected terms for all future presidents.

Soldiers remove Japanese Americans from their homes in California in 1942.

First Lady of the World

Eleanor Roosevelt was Theodore Roosevelt's niece and a distant cousin of Franklin's. She was active in her husband's political campaigns, especially after he got polio. As First Lady she became a powerful leader on her own, speaking out for the poor and for equal rights for women and African Americans. During the war, she traveled constantly in her husband's place, visiting the troops and America's allies. When she came home, she would leave notes for the president in a special "Eleanor basket" by his bedside. After Franklin's death, President Harry Truman named Eleanor one of America's first representatives to the United Nations, where she campaigned for human rights around the globe. Truman called her the "First Lady of the World."

The Atomic Bomb

Soon after Truman became president, Germany surrendered to America, Great Britain, and their allies. But Japan was still fighting. Truman now faced a difficult choice. Should he order an atomic bomb dropped on Japan? Before he took office, Truman knew nothing about the secret project to develop the powerful bomb. But after a July 1945 test, he knew what the weapon could do. Dropping one of these weapons on a Japanese city would certainly kill tens of thousands of people. But Truman thought hundreds of thousands of soldiers might die if the Allies had to invade Japan. On August 6, a U.S. bomber dropped an atomic bomb on Hiroshima, instantly killing 100,000 people. Japan didn't surrender, so a second bomb was dropped on the city of Nagasaki three days later. Japan ended the war the next day. Truman said he never regretted his decision.

BORN IN MISSOURI IN 1884; DIED IN 1972

When Franklin Roosevelt ran for his fourth term in 1944, he told voters, "Don't change horses midstream." He meant that they should keep the same president until World War II was over. Roosevelt won, but some voters believed that because of the president's poor health, his new vice president, Harry Truman, might have to take over. They were right. Just a few weeks after his fourth inauguration, Roosevelt died. When Truman heard the news, he asked Eleanor Roosevelt what he could do for her. She replied to the former senator from Missouri with the question, "Is there anything *we* can do for *you*? For *you* are the one in trouble now."

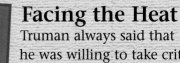

Facing the Heat

Truman always said that he was willing to take criticism. One of his favorite expressions was "If you can't stand the heat, get out of the kitchen." Another was "The buck stops here." He meant that he alone took responsibility for decisions made in his White House.

Harry S. Truman

U.S. Secretary of State Edward Stettinius signed the agreement forming the United Nations at a conference in San Francisco on June 26, 1945.

After the War

Following World War II, the United States joined the new United Nations, fulfilling Woodrow Wilson's dream of a world organization that would try to prevent war. At the same time, Truman worked with Congress to pass bills to help soldiers returning from the war find jobs and homes and complete their college educations. The United States also sent billions of dollars to European countries to help rebuild their cities.

The Cold War

The United States and the Soviet Union (formerly Russia) were allies during World War II, but quickly became rivals afterward. Their conflict was called the cold war, because the two countries never actually fought each other. But they did take opposite sides in several conflicts, including the Korean War.

DEWEY DEFEATS TRUMAN

After winning the 1948 election, Truman held up the front page of a Chicago newspaper that had been sure he would lose.

Surprise Election

In 1948, Truman ran for a full term as president against Governor Thomas Dewey of New York. Few people thought Truman could win, since the Democratic Party was divided. But Truman went on a long campaign trip, making 300 speeches across the nation. His work paid off, and he won a close race.

SMITHSONIAN LINK
Find out more about the end of World War II in Japan and see photos of the bombing of Hiroshima.
http://americanhistory.si.edu/militaryhistory/printable/section.asp?id=9&sub=8

Dwight D. Eisenhower
34TH PRESIDENT
1953–1961

BORN IN TEXAS IN 1890; DIED IN 1969

Dwight Eisenhower was a national hero after commanding the **Allied forces** in World War II and helping to plan the D-Day invasion of Europe, which helped end the war. In 1948, the Democrats asked him to run for president. He declined, instead running as a Republican four years later. His campaign slogan was "I Like Ike," because most Americans did. He easily won the 1952 election and was reelected in 1956. Although Eisenhower had been a soldier his entire career, he had no desire to lead the United States into war as president. "I hate war," he once said, "as only a soldier who has lived it can."

I LIKE IKE

The Little Rock Nine

In 1954, the Supreme Court ruled that states could not have separate public schools for different races. But some Southern states continued to segregate, or separate, the races in their schools. In 1957, the governor of Arkansas sent National Guard troops to Central High School in Little Rock to stop nine African-American students from entering. Eisenhower sent U.S. troops to the city to protect the students. It was a key moment in the fight to end segregation.

A Full Fifty

In 1959, when Alaska and Hawaii became the forty-ninth and fiftieth states, the United States took its current shape—183 years after the Declaration of Independence.

Camp David

Eisenhower was so fond of his grandson, David, that he named the presidential weekend house in the Maryland countryside Camp David. Presidents still use the 125-acre site for vacations and private meetings today.

U.S. soldiers drove the Little Rock Nine to Central High School to protect the students' safety.

John F. Kennedy
35TH PRESIDENT
1961–1963

BORN IN MASSACHUSETTS IN 1917;
DIED IN 1963

John Kennedy's father expected his oldest son, Joseph, to be president one day. But Joseph was killed in World War II. John was almost killed in the war too, when a Japanese ship smashed into his navy boat. But he survived and, in 1960, defeated Richard Nixon in one of the closest elections in history. Kennedy, who was forty-three, was the youngest man ever elected president.

Kennedy and Soviet leader Khrushchev met in Europe in 1961. A year later, their countries almost went to war.

Challenging Americans

The new president told Americans, "Ask not what your country can do for you—ask what you can do for your country." Many young people responded by joining the Peace Corps, a new program that sent Americans to help people in poor countries. Kennedy also challenged Americans to beat the Soviet Union in the "space race" to the moon by the end of the 1960s. They did. In 1969, U.S. astronauts were the first to walk on the moon.

Missiles in Cuba

In October 1962, the world came close to a nuclear war, a war in which atomic weapons would be used. The United States discovered that the Soviet Union was building a nuclear missile base in Cuba, just ninety miles from Florida. Kennedy sent navy ships to block routes to the island and demanded that Soviet leader Nikita Khrushchev remove the missiles. After several tense days, Kennedy and Khrushchev reached a deal, to the relief of the world.

Murder in Dallas

On November 22, 1963, while riding through Dallas in an open car next to his wife, Jacqueline, Kennedy was shot and killed by a gunman. Just hours later, Mrs. Kennedy stood beside new president Lyndon Johnson as he took the oath of office.

SMITHSONIAN LINK
Learn more about First Lady Jacqueline Kennedy and see the gown she wore to her husband's inauguration.
http://historywired.si.edu/object.cfm?ID=311

Lyndon B. Johnson
36TH PRESIDENT
1963–1969

BORN IN TEXAS IN 1908; DIED IN 1973

Lyndon Baines Johnson always had great influence on people. When he married Claudia Taylor, whose nickname was "Lady Bird," her initials became LBJ, just like his. The couple named their daughters Lynda Bird and Luci Baines and their dogs Little Beagle Johnson and Little Beagle Junior, so they would have the same set of initials too.

The Great Society

Johnson worked with Congress to make laws ending poverty and racism. He called this program the Great Society. Head Start preschools were part of it. So were Medicare and Medicaid, which helped the elderly and the poor pay medical bills. Johnson also signed the Civil Rights Act of 1964, banning segregation in public places and making it illegal for companies to refuse to hire people because of their race. The Voting Rights Act of 1965 made it illegal for states to force any American to pass a test before voting. (Unfair tests had been used in some states to keep African Americans from voting.) Johnson also chose the first African-American Supreme Court justice, Thurgood Marshall. Before he became a judge, Marshall had argued as a lawyer in front of the Court in the case that ruled that school segregation was illegal.

War in Vietnam

A small number of American troops had been in South Vietnam for several years, helping that government fight off an invasion from North Vietnam. As the fighting heated up, Johnson sent more troops. By 1968, there were almost 500,000 Americans in Vietnam, and no end in sight to the war. Millions of Americans began to protest the war and demand that Johnson pull out U.S. troops.

Hundreds of thousands of Americans joined the peace movement and went to protests and rallies urging the president to take U.S. troops out of Vietnam.

61

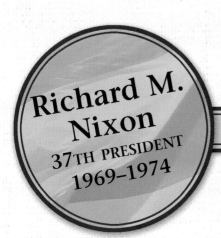

BORN IN CALIFORNIA IN 1913; DIED IN 1994

As a young man, Richard Nixon was quiet and serious and did not make friends easily. He was still able to have a successful career in politics, and became Dwight Eisenhower's vice president at age thirty-nine. But after losing elections for president in 1960 and for California governor in 1962, he quit politics, saying, "You won't have Nixon to kick around anymore." Then, in 1968, he made an amazing comeback.

The 1968 Election

After completing Kennedy's term, Lyndon Johnson easily won election in 1964. But by 1968, the war in Vietnam had made him so unpopular that he chose not to run again. John Kennedy's younger brother Robert was a leading Democratic candidate. But on the night Robert Kennedy won the California primary, he was **assassinated**. Hubert Humphrey became the nominee instead, but lost the election to the Republican, Nixon.

Out of Vietnam

During the 1968 campaign, Nixon told voters he had a "secret plan" to take U.S. troops out of Vietnam. As president, he increased bombing of North Vietnam and tried to replace American soldiers with South Vietnamese troops. A peace agreement was finally signed in 1973. It called for U.S. combat troops to leave the region but allowed South Vietnam to keep some territory it had captured.

The president and First Lady Pat Nixon strolled along the Great Wall of China during their 1972 visit.

World Traveler

As a member of Congress from 1946 to 1952, Nixon had led an investigation into whether spies from the Soviet Union and China were working in the U.S. government. So Americans were shocked when President Nixon decided to travel to both of those countries in 1972. Nixon reached no new agreements with Chinese leaders during his trip. However, they had friendly discussions, and China soon sent a pair of rare giant pandas to the National Zoo in Washington, D.C., as a gift to the United States. Later that year, in the Soviet capital, Moscow, Nixon and Soviet leaders agreed to set new limits on nuclear weapons.

Watergate

On June 17, 1972, burglars broke into national Democratic Party offices in the Watergate building in Washington. One of the burglars worked for Nixon's Committee to Re-elect the President. The president told reporters he knew nothing about the break-in and easily won reelection later that year. But people kept asking questions.

Nixon gave a "victory" salute to staff members as he boarded a helicopter to leave the White House after he resigned on August 9, 1974.

A President Quits

In February 1973, a special Senate committee began looking into the break-in, by then part of a larger scandal simply known as Watergate. One senator asked, "What did the President know, and when did he know it?" When a presidential staff member told the committee that Nixon secretly recorded all of his White House conversations, the Senate demanded the tapes. Nixon refused to turn them over. Soon, for the first time since Andrew Johnson's term, Congress prepared to impeach the president. In July 1974, the Supreme Court ruled that Nixon had to hand over his tapes, and on August 5, Nixon released conversations from 1972 that proved he lied to cover up the break-in. On August 9, he became the only president in American history to resign from office. "I let the American people down," he said.

Gerald R. Ford
38TH PRESIDENT
1974–1977

BORN IN NEBRASKA IN 1913; DIED IN 2006

After a televised stumble and skits making fun of him on the new TV show *Saturday Night Live*, President Gerald Ford got a reputation for being clumsy. In fact, Ford had been a fashion model and a college football star, and was also a fine golfer and swimmer.

Getting over Nixon

Nixon's first vice president, Spiro Agnew, had resigned in 1973, and Nixon chose Ford to replace him. As a result, when Nixon resigned, Ford became the first president who had never been elected either as vice president or president. In his new job, Ford promised to restore confidence in the presidency. "Our long national nightmare is over," he said. But it really wasn't, because it was still possible that Nixon could be charged with crimes and go on trial. Ford believed that, if this happened, it could distract the nation for years. So he used his presidential powers to pardon Nixon, or excuse him from going on trial.

A Strong First Lady

Former dancer Betty Ford became an especially popular First Lady. After battling breast cancer, she spoke out to raise awareness of the disease. After leaving the White House, Mrs. Ford admitted to abusing alcohol and painkilling drugs, and helped to found the country's most famous clinic for the treatment of addiction, the Betty Ford Center.

Ford welcomes South Vietnamese orphans arriving in the United States after the airlift.

The End of the War

American troops officially left Vietnam in 1973, and North Vietnam completed its invasion of South Vietnam two years later, in April 1975. U.S. helicopters rushed to lift 7,000 people, including 1,400 Americans, out of the southern capital, Saigon, before it fell to northern troops. The helicopters lifted the people off the grounds of the U.S. embassy just before it was captured.

BORN IN GEORGIA IN 1924

Democrats were sure that Ford's pardon of Nixon would keep him from winning the 1976 election. Fourteen candidates entered the field for the party's nomination. Georgia governor Jimmy Carter, who once ran his family's peanut business, was one of the least known. But he won the nomination, and then defeated Ford in a close election.

Hostages in Iran

In 1979, a revolution forced Iran's king, known as the shah, to escape the country. The shah came to America later that year for cancer treatments. On November 4, a group of students attacked the U.S. embassy in Iran, took staff members hostage, and demanded that Carter return the shah to their country. The president refused. As months went by, he was unable to negotiate the hostages' release. Finally, after 444 days, the fifty-two hostages were set free on the day Carter left office. His failure to free them earlier contributed to his loss in the 1980 election.

Former American hostages wave to supporters after their flight out of Iran.

Carter brought together Egyptian president Anwar Sadat, left, and Israeli prime minister Menachem Begin.

History at Camp David

Carter achieved a stunning success when he negotiated a peace treaty between Israel and Egypt. The Middle Eastern neighbors had been bitter enemies since Israel was founded in 1948, but after meeting with Carter for thirteen straight days at Camp David, their leaders signed a historic agreement in 1978.

After the White House

Carter proved to be one of the most active former presidents in history. The projects he started include building houses for the homeless and speaking out for peace and human rights around the world. In 2002, he won the Nobel Peace Prize.

Ronald Reagan
40TH PRESIDENT
1981–1989

BORN IN ILLINOIS IN 1911; DIED IN 2004

Before he entered politics, Ronald Reagan had a successful career as an actor. He appeared in more than fifty movies as well as several TV shows. He met his second wife, Nancy, who was an actress, when they worked together on a film. His ability to appear comfortable and confident when speaking on TV earned him the nickname the "Great Communicator."

An Illegal Deal
In 1986, journalists discovered that White House officials had secretly sold weapons to Iran. Iran used the weapons in its war with Iraq. In return, Iran helped to win the release of American hostages in Lebanon. Money from the weapons sale was then sent to help rebel fighters in the Central American country of Nicaragua, whose government opposed the United States. Congress, however, had outlawed American aid to the rebels. Reagan insisted that he knew nothing about the illegal deals made by members of his staff.

Power to the Vice President
The economy was not strong during much of Reagan's time in office. Still, the president remained popular and was reelected in 1984, partly because he had cut taxes. In 1988, Vice President George H. W. Bush ran for president, promising to continue Reagan's tax policies. He said, "Read my lips: no new taxes," and became the first vice president since Martin Van Buren elected by voters to follow his president into office.

A Farewell to America
At age sixty-nine, Reagan was the oldest man ever elected president. He was seventy-eight when he left office after two terms. While Reagan was president, he admitted to having a poor memory; but after he left office, doctors discovered that he suffered from Alzheimer's disease, which sometimes causes people to lose their memories almost completely. In 1994, as Reagan's mind began to fail, he released a handwritten farewell letter to Americans. Reagan's honest message brought new attention to the disease. "I now begin the journey that will lead me into the sunset of my life," he wrote. Reagan died ten years later.

A police officer and a Secret Service agent were injured when a gunman opened fire on Reagan. Press secretary James Brady was shot in the head and suffered permanent brain damage.

A Survivor
Just a few weeks into Reagan's first term as president, a gunman shot him in Washington, D.C. But the bullet just missed the president's heart, and he made a full recovery. In the hospital, he told doctors, "I forgot to duck."

Reagan and Soviet leader Gorbachev shake hands at the start of their White House meeting.

An End to the Cold War?

Reagan said he wanted to protect the United States from its cold war rival, the Soviet Union, which he called an "evil empire." Congress supported his plans to spend billions of dollars on new weapons, including research into a system of satellites in space that were supposed to shoot down enemy missiles. That program, nicknamed "Star Wars," was never built. Later, during Reagan's second term, he met with a new Soviet leader, Mikhail Gorbachev, who was working to change his country's government. After friendly talks, the two men signed a historic agreement to cut the number of nuclear weapons in each country.

George H. W. Bush
41ST PRESIDENT
1989–1993

BORN IN MASSACHUSETTS IN 1924

When World War II began, George Bush was eager to serve. As soon as he turned eighteen, he joined the navy and quickly became its youngest pilot. Bush flew fifty-eight combat missions in the war, many of them in a bomber plane he named *Barbara*, after the girlfriend who became his wife and First Lady.

Changes in Europe

The changes Mikhail Gorbachev brought to the Soviet government led to big changes in Europe. Under Gorbachev, the Soviet Union gave up control of the governments of several Eastern European countries. In 1990, East Germany (which had been under Soviet control since the end of World War II) reunited with West Germany. With the cold war finally over, Russian and American leaders began to work together, in what President Bush called a "new world order."

War with Iraq

In 1990, Saddam Hussein, leader of Iraq, ordered an invasion of his country's smaller neighbor, Kuwait, which has one of the world's largest supplies of oil. Bush worked with the United Nations to put together a group of allies to oppose Hussein. When Iraq refused to leave Kuwait, soldiers from the United States and its allies launched a war that forced Hussein's soldiers back to Iraq within six weeks. Twelve years later, though, American troops would return to fight in Iraq again.

Helping people learn to read was important to the First Lady, who wrote a children's book, *Millie's Book*, about the Bush family dog.

The president spent Thanksgiving with U.S. troops in Saudi Arabia in 1990.

First Lady and First Mother

When her son George W. Bush was elected president in 2000, Barbara Bush became the only woman besides Abigail Adams to be the wife of one president and the mother of another.

***BORN IN ARKANSAS
IN 1946***

In 1963, teenager Bill Clinton traveled to Washington for a national conference of high school students. At a visit to the White House, he shook hands with his hero, John F. Kennedy. Clinton later said that day changed his life, convincing him to go into politics instead of becoming a professional saxophone player.

The new president played his saxophone at a celebration of his first inauguration in 1993.

Bombing at the World Trade Center

In 1993, a group of Muslim terrorists tried to blow up New York City's World Trade Center by driving a van full of explosives into a garage under the two giant office buildings. They failed, but the buildings remained a target for terrorists. Clinton ordered the military to locate and attack the terrorist leaders living outside the United States who had ordered the bombing.

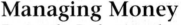

Six people were killed, and more than 1,000 were injured, in the 1993 blast beneath the World Trade Center.

Managing Money

During the Bush years, there was a downturn in the country's economy, many people lost their jobs, and the government collected much less in taxes than it needed to spend. President Bush had to go back on his campaign promise not to raise taxes. During the 1992 election, Bush said that the economy would improve soon. Voters didn't believe him— and Bush lost the election to Clinton—but Bush was right about the economy. Under Clinton, the economy boomed. Individuals and companies began earning more money, and the government collected billions of dollars more than it needed to spend.

William Clinton

Terror at Home

In 1995, terrorists destroyed a government office building in Oklahoma City, Oklahoma, killing 168 people. At the time, it was the worst terrorist attack ever in the United States. Police captured two men involved in the bombing. They were Americans who hated the government.

Clinton met with three former presidents at the White House in 1993: Jimmy Carter, Gerald Ford, and George H.W. Bush.

First Lady of the Senate

Before moving to the White House, Hillary Clinton was a successful lawyer with political dreams of her own. In November 2000, near the end of her husband's second term, she was elected U.S. senator from New York, making her the only First Lady ever elected to a national office. In 2008, she ran for president herself.

Clashes with Congress

In the Congressional elections of 1994, halfway into Clinton's first term, voters took control of both the House of Representatives and the Senate away from his Democratic Party. After this midterm election loss, the president often argued with Republicans in Congress over how the nation should spend its money. Twice, government offices had to shut down because Clinton and Congress couldn't agree on a spending plan. Despite those problems, voters elected the president to a second term in 1996.

Rivals Become Friends

In 2004, President George W. Bush asked his father to work with former president Bill Clinton to raise money to help people in Asia and Africa recover from a terrible earthquake and a huge sea wave called a tsunami. To the surprise of many Americans, the two former presidents became close friends while working together.

SMITHSONIAN LINK
See what a modern inauguration looks like, including the fireworks, in a set of photographs from President Clinton's first inauguration.
http://photo2.si.edu/inaugural/clinton1/clinton1.html

BORN IN CONNECTICUT IN 1946

The 2000 election between Texas governor George W. Bush and Vice President Al Gore was one of the closest ever. The race in Florida was especially close. State officials said Bush had won, but Democrats demanded a recount. Eventually, the Supreme Court had to settle the dispute. In a 5–4 vote, the justices ordered Florida officials to stop recounting the ballots, giving the election to Bush.

War in Iraq

In 2003, Bush told Americans that dictator Saddam Hussein of Iraq was secretly trying to build nuclear weapons—and was working with Al Qaeda. Both of these claims would prove to be incorrect, but not before Congress approved an invasion of Iraq. Some Americans opposed the idea from the beginning. U.S. troops quickly forced Hussein out of office. But as rival groups inside Iraq began to fight one another, Americans were caught in the middle of a civil war.

September 11

On September 11, 2001, terrorists took over four jet planes, crashing two into the towers of New York's World Trade Center and one into the Pentagon building near Washington, D.C., home of the U.S. Department of Defense. The fourth plane crashed in a Pennsylvania field. Nearly three thousand people died in the attacks, which were carried out by the terrorist group Al Qaeda, led by Osama bin Laden.

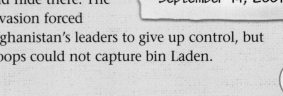

The War on Terror

After the attacks, President Bush sent U.S. troops into Afghanistan, because that country's leaders had allowed members of Al Qaeda to train and hide there. The invasion forced Afghanistan's leaders to give up control, but troops could not capture bin Laden.

The president visited New York City firefighters at the site of the fallen World Trade Center on September 14, 2001.

U.S. soldiers on patrol near Baghdad, Iraq, in 2003

Presidential Extremes

America's presidents have been large and small, thin and fat, young and old. Which presidents are the most extreme? Check the facts below.

TALLEST PRESIDENT:
Abraham Lincoln (1861–1865) was 6 feet 4 inches tall.

SHORTEST PRESIDENT:
James Madison (1809–1817) was only 5 feet 4 inches tall.

LIGHTEST PRESIDENT:
James Madison (1809–1817) weighed only about 100 pounds.

President with the shortest term in office:
William Henry Harrison (1841) served thirty-one days before he died of pneumonia.

William Harrison was president for only a month, but his grandson Benjamin later served a full four-year term.

PRESIDENT WITH THE LONGEST TERM IN OFFICE:
Franklin D. Roosevelt (1933–1945) served for twelve years, one month, and eight days before he died in office.

YOUNGEST PRESIDENT:
Theodore Roosevelt (1901–1909) was only forty-two when he took office after William McKinley's death.

Despite his weight, President Taft enjoyed playing baseball. He was the first president to throw out the first ball at the start of the major-league season.

YOUNGEST ELECTED PRESIDENT:
John Kennedy (1961–1963) was forty-three when he took office after winning the 1960 election.

OLDEST ELECTED PRESIDENT:
Ronald Reagan (1981–1989) was sixty-nine when he took office.

ONLY PRESIDENT NEVER TO MARRY:
James Buchanan (1857–1861) asked his niece to perform some of the duties of First Lady.

Heaviest president:
William Howard Taft (1909–1913) weighed more than 300 pounds.

The headquarters of the Department of Housing and Urban Development is called the Robert C. Weaver Federal Building, after HUD's first secretary.

BIRTHPLACE OF THE MOST PRESIDENTS:
Eight presidents were born in Virginia. Seven were born in Ohio.

ONLY PRESIDENT ELECTED UNANIMOUSLY:
George Washington (1789–1797) received every vote in the Electoral College. James Monroe (1817–1825) received every vote except one in 1820. A New Hampshire elector did not want anyone to tie Washington's record.

First president to live in the White House:
John Adams (1797–1801) and his family moved into the mansion in 1800, even though it wasn't completely finished.

President who chose the first African-American cabinet member:
Lyndon B. Johnson (1963–1969) named Robert Weaver the first secretary of housing and urban development (HUD) in 1966.

SIGNERS OF THE DECLARATION OF INDEPENDENCE:
John Adams (1797–1801) and Thomas Jefferson (1801–1809) were the only presidents to sign the Declaration.

PRESIDENT WHO CHOSE THE FIRST HISPANIC CABINET MEMBER:
Ronald Reagan (1981–1989) named Lauro Cavazos secretary of education in 1988.

PRESIDENT WHO CHOSE THE FIRST WOMAN CABINET MEMBER:
Franklin D. Roosevelt (1933–1945) named Frances Perkins secretary of labor in 1933.

ONLY PET TO SERVE TWO PRESIDENTS:
Spot, a springer spaniel, was born in the White House when George H. W. Bush (1989–1993) was president. He returned to the White House with George W. Bush in 2001.

Adams was upset that the White House was not finished before his family moved in on November 1, 1800. The Adamses dried their laundry in the massive East Room.

James G. Barber

Historian, National Portrait Gallery,
Smithsonian Institution

Why did you become a historian?
For much of my life I have lived on land
once owned by George Washington.
Since I live near Mount Vernon in northern Virginia, where a lot of history has
taken place, I have always been curious
about the people, places, and events that
have shaped our heritage.

**What incident or person from your
childhood influenced your decision?**
Family trips to historic places like
Williamsburg, Virginia, and Gettysburg,
Pennsylvania, were always interesting
learning adventures for me. At an early
age I could see myself someday working
in a museum or at a historic site.

**How can kids get interested in
your field?**
Good books, field trips to historic places,
interactive websites, and teachers are
excellent ways to become introduced to
the subject.

**What do you do most of the time?
What do you do every day?**
My work involves a lot of reading and

writing, which I do every day. The
museum exhibition work that I do now
involves researching, writing, and selecting pertinent objects for museum displays and book illustrations.

**What are the most important quali-
ties for an expert in your field?**
In a history museum, which displays
historical paintings and photographs, it
is important to be able to look carefully
at old pictures for clues about their
authenticity and origin. For instance,
oftentimes the signatures with which
artists signed their paintings are not
always legible at first glance. But if
compared with known signatures on
other paintings, the correct name can
sometimes be discovered, with a lot of
perseverance and a little luck.

**What is the biggest recent discovery
in your field?**
One example might be the "possible"
identification of the earliest known photo-
graph of Mathew Brady, the famous Civil
War photographer. I am saying "possible"
because this potential discovery is still
being investigated and may never be

proven to be true. There is much in history that is unknown and will always remain unknown for lack of documentation and physical evidence.

Is there something in your field you wish was studied more?

Portraits of the presidents could always be studied progressively and in greater detail. President Lincoln was an excellent example of a president who took the time and allowed himself to be photographed throughout the years of his presidency. Consequently, the visual record of him is quite good and shows clearly how he aged in office.

What do you like most about your job?

Imagine being able to relive the life of a historical figure such as Theodore Roosevelt by creating an exhibition of artifacts that he once owned. Those possessions might include his cowboy hat and guns, his Rough Rider uniform, and perhaps even wild animals such as a lion and a water buffalo that he hunted in Africa and brought home with him and had preserved.

What was the most exciting discovery you ever made?

After studying what I thought were *all* of the painted portraits of President Andrew Jackson that were done from life (with Jackson sitting in front of the artist), it was exciting to have discovered, while on a vacation, yet another life portrait, this one hanging in a hotel lobby in Charleston, South Carolina.

What are some of the most unusual objects in the Smithsonian collection you work with?

The Smithsonian once borrowed folk portraits of presidents from the presidential libraries for an exhibition at the National Portrait Gallery. They included a portrait of President Reagan made with jelly beans, a carved peach-pit portrait of President Kennedy, a carved matchstick portrait of President Nixon, and a papier-mâché peanut bearing President Carter's trademark toothy smile. Many of these wacky images were made by children and sent to the presidents as gifts.

Have you ever met a president?

I once met and shook hands with the first President Bush at a White House reception.

What is an interesting fact that most people don't know about our presidents?

Eight presidents were born in Virginia, more than in any other state. Seven of the eight were born less than a hundred miles from each other, and three—Washington, Madison, and Monroe—were born less than twenty miles apart.

Glossary

agency—A department of the government focused on a specific area, like agriculture or military defense.

Allied forces—In World War II, the Allied forces were made up of the United States, Great Britain, China, the Soviet Union, and more than forty other countries.

assassinate—To murder a president or other political leader.

Bill of Rights—The first ten amendments (or additions) to the U.S. Constitution, which guarantee many of the basic rights of American citizens.

cabinet—Officials chosen by the president to be advisers and to lead major departments in the government's executive branch.

checks and balances—A system that balances power among the branches—executive, legislative, and judicial—of the U.S. government.

civil service—The system of government jobs.

commission—A group within the government given special powers to perform a specific duty.

Congress—The legislative (law-making) branch of the United States government, which has two houses—the House of Representatives and the Senate—each with representatives from all fifty states.

Constitution—The U.S. Constitution is the country's supreme law and the plan for its national government. It became law in 1789.

convention—A meeting of a political party for the purpose of selecting candidates for office.

draft—The selection of young men from the populace for the purpose of serving in the military.

Electoral College—The official body, made up of electors from each state, that elects the president of the United States.

era—An important period in the history of a country.

executive branch—The branch of the U.S. government, led by the president, that enforces the law.

House of Representatives—The house of Congress in which each state's number of representatives is based on its population.

impeach—To charge a president or other government official with wrongdoing, or to try to remove an official from office.

inauguration—The swearing-in ceremony in which a president officially takes office.

internment camp—A place where a government confines people who are considered to be suspicious, especially during a war.

manifest destiny—The popular belief in the 1800s that the United States was meant to stretch west to the Pacific Ocean and south to the Rio Grande.

nominate—To choose someone to run for office, or to be appointed to a government job.

nominee—A political party's choice as candidate for an election.

political party—A large group of people who share similar ideas about government.

primary election—An election in which members of a political party choose its nominee for president or other office.

secede—To break away from a group, as Southern states broke away from the United States in 1861.

self-evident—Obvious or clear to anyone.

Senate—The house of Congress in which each of the fifty states has two representatives.

spoils system—The practice of giving important public offices to the members of the winning political party after an election.

territory—An area of land, not yet a state, that is controlled by a nation.

third-party candidate—A candidate from a party other than the Democratic or Republican Party.

treaty—A formal agreement between two or more countries.

trust—A company or group of companies that controls a certain industry without competition.

veto—To refuse to sign, or approve, a law.

More to See and Read

Websites

There are links to many wonderful web pages below. But the web is constantly growing and changing, so we cannot guarantee that the sites we recommend will be available when you go online. If the site you want is no longer there, you can always find information about the presidents, and a great learning experience, through the main Smithsonian website: www.si.edu.

To find out more about each president, try these sites:
www.smithsonianeducation.org/president/index.htm
www.whitehouse.gov/history/presidents
www.npg.si.edu
www.civilwar.si.edu

To view exhibits from the Smithsonian Institution about each president, see:
http://americanhistory.si.edu/presidency/home.html

To read more about the history of the White House, try:
www.whitehouse.gov/history/life

To find out more about how presidents get elected, go to:
http://bensguide.gpo.gov/6-8/election/primary.html

To learn more about the job of the Secret Service, visit:
www.secretservice.gov/faq.shtml or www.secretservice.gov/kids_faq.shtml

To find out about presidential libraries and museums that you can visit, go to:
www.archives.gov/presidential-libraries

Suggested Reading

The White House: An Illustrated History by Catherine O. Grace.

Air Force One: The Aircraft that Shaped the Modern Presidency by Von Hardesty.

Lives of the Presidents: Fame, Shame (and What the Neighbors Thought) by Kathleen Krull.

The Smithsonian Book of the First Ladies: Their Lives, Times, and Issues edited by Edith P. Mayo.

So You Want to be President? by Judith St. George.

How to Be President: What to Do and Where to Go Once You're in Office by Stephen P. Williams.

Index